LIFE OF CRABBE.

LIFE

OF

GEORGE CRABBE

BY

T. E. KEBBEL, M.A.

KENNIKAT PRESS
Port Washington, N. Y./London

LIFE OF GEORGE CRABBE

First published in 1888
Reissued in 1972 by Kennikat Press
Library of Congress Catalog Card No: 70-160764
ISBN 0-8046-1584-5

Manufactured by Taylor Publishing Company   Dallas, Texas

CONTENTS.

———◆———

CHAPTER I.

CHAPTER II.

CHAPTER III.

CHAPTER IV.

CHAPTER V.

CHAPTER VI.

CHAPTER VII.

CHAPTER VIII.

NOTE.

ALMOST all the sources of information available for a life of Crabbe at the date of his death were exhausted by his son, the Rev. George Crabbe, in writing his father's biography, which must always remain the standard work upon the subject. This was published in 1834, and since that time has gone through several editions. Besides what is founded on the autobiographical memoirs, contributed by Crabbe himself to the *New Monthly Magazine* to accompany his own portrait, it contains the reminiscences of Moore, Campbell, Lockhart, Mrs. Joanna Baillie, and her friend, Mr. Duncan, a sketch communicated by Mr. Taylor, of Trowbridge, one of Crabbe's parishioners, and a good deal of Crabbe's correspondence with Mary Leadbeater, of whom some account will be found in the following pages. A short sketch of him has been written by the Rev..Mr. Bransby, of Carnarvon, and a very good one by Mr. Bernard Barton in his *Historic Sites of Suffolk*, published in 1841, together with an engraving of the house at Aldeburgh in which Crabbe was born, a mere cottage, since swept away by the sea. I am also indebted to Mr. Leslie Stephen's article on Crabbe in the " Dictionary of National Biography ; " and I should also mention Mr. W. J. Courthope's interesting little notice prefixed to the selections from Crabbe in Mr. Ward's "English Poets ;" which, however, I had not read before my own work was finished. Through the kindness of the Duke and Duchess of Rutland, I have been able to glean some further particulars of Crabbe's residence in Leicestershire, and only regret that my stay at Belvoir was too short to admit of my visiting Croxton Kyriel, the scene of Crabbe's botanising expeditions when he was chaplain at the castle. To the Rev. James Furnival, the Rector of Muston, I am indebted for many interesting little circumstances, which will also be found in the following pages ; while, in Miss Crowfoot of Beccles, I have had the pleasure of conversing with a lady who remembers Crabbe well, and who, when a girl of eighteen, used to stay with him at Trowbridge Rectory. Miss Crowfoot is a cousin of the lady who married Crabbe's son, the author of the Biography, and to her I am indebted for the account of the poet's descendants.

T. E. K.

LIFE OF CRABBE.

CHAPTER I.

GEORGE CRABBE was born at Aldeburgh, in Suffolk, on the 24th of December 1754. Aldeburgh, now become a fashionable watering-place, was then, according to the Biography,* though it returned two members to Parliament, "a poor and wretched place, consisting of two parallel and unpaved streets, running between mean and scrambling houses, the abodes of sea-faring men, pilots, and fishers." Much of the old town had already been washed away by the sea, and Crabbe himself, so late as January 1779, saw eleven houses destroyed at once by an unusually high spring-tide. The house in which Crabbe was born stood in this row of buildings, the upper rooms projecting far over the ground floor, and the windows, with old-fashioned diamond panes, hardly admitting the light of day. The scenery all round was then what it is now; but of that the description must be sought in the poet's own verses.

* The references throughout to the Poet's Biography are references to his Life by his son. — *Vide Prefatory Note.*

Crabbe is, or was, a well-known name among the wealthier class of Norfolk yeomen, but is not found among the gentry. The son, indeed, tells us of an old coat-of-arms preserved by his uncle at Southwold; but as nobody could tell how it came into the possession of the family, they very sensibly declined to found any aristocratic pretensions on it. The poet's grandfather was a burgess of Aldeburgh, and Collector of Customs. His son kept the village school at Orford, and afterwards at Norton, near Loddon, in Norfolk, where he was also parish-clerk; and to these experiences the poet was, no doubt, indebted for some touches in the "Parish Register" and the "Borough." The elder Crabbe returned to Aldeburgh about the year 1750; and soon afterwards married Mrs. Loddock, a widow, of that town, where he finally settled, and obtained the office of Saltmaster, or collector of the salt duties. He was a man of some education, fond of English literature, and a good mathematician. The sketch of the learned schoolmaster in the "Borough" may have been in part suggested to Crabbe by his father's reminiscences. In the evenings he would sometimes read aloud Young or Milton to the family circle, and he frequently, we are told, used to solace his irksome labours with Pope, Milton, and Dryden. Thus we see that young Crabbe, in spite of the roughness and coarseness of the class with which he necessarily associated, was brought up in a comparatively intellectual atmosphere; and he seems very early to have given signs that nature had intended him for something better than the society of "the wild amphibious race" who owned or manned the Aldeburgh fishing-boats, or worked in the warehouses on Slaugden Quay, a suburb of Aldeburgh, where the river Alde empties itself into the sea. The boy's father, besides his official duties, had a share in the industries of the place, and was part-owner of a fishing-boat. He at first designed his eldest son for the same occupation, but soon found out that he was never likely to make a seaman. "That boy," he would say, "must be a fool. John and Bob and Will are all of some use about a boat, but what will that *thing* ever be good for?"

At a very early age Crabbe began to try to write verses in imitation of those which he found in the Poet's Corner of *Martin's Philosophical Magazine*, a periodical taken in by his father, who, when he sent the volumes to be bound, used to cut out and throw away these effusions. George picked them up, and from that time forward was a poet. The literary taste which he then unconsciously imbibed led him to search in the cottages of the fishermen for old ballads or books, which he sometimes read out to them in the winter evenings, and he grew by degrees to be a great favourite with their wives and daughters. His character became known, and he already began to be respected. Once when he had been unlucky enough to quarrel in the street with a boy much bigger than himself, another interfered to protect him, on the ground that he "had got larning." This occurred, as we are given to understand, before he went to his first school. Crabbe at the time could have been little more than six years old—about the same age as Pope was when he first "became a lover of books." His father, instead of checking him roughly for such propensities, as many in his position would have done, resolved to give them fair-play, and sent him, at seven years of age, to a school at Bungay, a village near Great Yarmouth, where the room he used to sleep in may still be seen by the inquisitive. Few anecdotes of his early school life have been preserved; but one of his school-fellows loved to tell in after-life, when Crabbe had become famous, how, on the first Sunday morning after his arrival, he appealed to him to help him with his dress. " Please, Master ——, will you help me to put on my collar?" And the biographer, who tells the above story in another form, adds, that on one occasion he narrowly escaped suffocation. " He and several of his school-fellows were punished for playing at soldiers, by being put into a large dog-kennel, known by the terrible name of 'the Black Hole.' George was the first that entered : and the place being crammed full with offenders, the atmosphere soon became pestilentially close. The poor boy in vain shrieked that he was about to be suffocated. At last, in despair, he bit the lad next to him violently in the hand. 'Crabbe is dying—Crabbe is dying!' roared the sufferer ; and the sentinel at length opened the door and allowed the boys to rush out in the air. My father said, a minute more and I must have died."

The second school to which he was sent was kept by a Mr. Richard Haddon, at Stow Market, under whom Crabbe made great progress in mathematics, and acquired a fair knowledge of the classics. It is related that Crabbe senior used sometimes to send problems to Mr. Haddon, and, greatly to the father's delight, they were frequently answered by his son. If tradition can be trusted, it was here too that his talent for satire first shewed itself, as he is reputed to have written a copy of verses on one of the female scholars who used to attend the writing-school, warning her against thinking too much of the blue ribbons in her bonnet.

It was now resolved that Crabbe should adopt surgery as a profession ; and he remained at home for some time before a situation could be found for him. It was during this interval, when he was about thirteen, that he occupied himself as described in the *Tales of the Hall*, wandering along the sandy and marshy tracts, with their stunted trees and scant herbage, which form the sea-board of the eastern counties, watching the sea-gulls and curlews, talking to the superstitious old shepherds on the heath, or even penetrating to the Smugglers' Cave. At other times he would give his whole attention to the busy scenes presented by the town, talking with the tradesmen in their shops, with the sailors on the beach, observing the signals from the ships at sea, and, whatever was going forward, never resting, as he says, till he knew what it meant, and the reason for everything that was done. In his " Office and Work of Universities," Cardinal Newman says of the passage in which this period of the poet's life is described, that "it is one of the most touching in our language." "I read it," he adds, "on its first publication, above thirty years ago, with extreme delight, and have never lost my love for it ; and on looking it up lately, found I was even more touched by it than heretofore. A work which can please in youth and age seems to fulfil (in logical language) the accidental definition of a classic."

During the interval that elapsed between Crabbe's return to Aldeburgh and his being bound apprentice to a surgeon, he was again set to work upon the Quay, and again displayed the same impatience of its monotonous and

laborious drudgery. He did not gain much, however, by
his transfer, in 1768, to a surgery at Wickham-Brook,
where his master employed him rather as an errand-boy
than assistant, compelled him to sleep with the ploughman, and sometimes to work upon the farm. It is said
that on his first arrival he was much mortified by the
daughter of the house bursting out laughing at him,
exclaiming at the same time, in a tone of anything but
admiration, " La! here's our new apprentice!" At this
time he often carried medicines to Chevely, and little
thought that in a few short years he would be an inmate
of the Hall, and sitting at the Duke of Rutland's
table. In 1771 he obtained a more agreeable situation
with Mr. Page, a surgeon at Woodbridge, where he
found companions of his own age, and began to feel
himself a man. He joined a village club, which used
to meet once-a-week at an inn, for discussion of
the subjects in which the members were interested,
and here he made friends which influenced his future
life.

One was a young man named Levet, then engaged
to be married to a Miss Brereton of Framlingham; the
young lady's most intimate friend being a Miss Elmy,
who lived with her uncle, Mr. Tovel, in the village of
Parham. Levet one day asked Crabbe to be his companion in a visit to Parham, where Miss Brereton was
then staying. He agreed, and being then and there
introduced to Miss Elmy, fell in love with her at once,
and seems not to have been long before he told her
so. This was in 1772, when Crabbe was not yet
eighteen, while Miss Elmy was nearly two-and-twenty.
In ordinary cases a girl of this age regards a lad of

eighteen as a mere boy, whom she may indulge in
a juvenile flirtation, but would never think seriously
of marrying. Miss Elmy, however, seems at once
to have accepted his addresses; and we might almost
infer from this that she was the first to detect the
real genius which lay hidden under the mean exterior
of the poor surgeon's apprentice, then in a position
scarcely above the rank of a menial. Her own family,
though now in reduced circumstances, had usually ranked
as gentlefolks; and the uncle, a wealthy old yeoman, with
whom she lived at Parham, never disguised, even in
Crabbe's presence, his contempt for literature, and all
belonging to it. He reflected probably, with old
Osborne in "Vanity Fair," that he could "buy up the
beggarly hounds twice over." "That damned learning,"
as he called it, was the frequent object of his sneers;
and brought up in such an atmosphere as this, it is clear
that Miss Elmy must have possessed unusual strength
of mind and knowledge of character, not only to
accept Crabbe while he was still in the position I have
described, but also, instead of advising him either to
stick steadily to his profession, or to go into business
with his father, to encourage his poetical aspirations,
and prompt him to write verses when he ought to have
been mixing medicines.

It was in the year 1772 that he gained the prize offered
by Wheble, the editor of the *Lady's Magazine*, for a
poem on "Hope," of which the extract given in the
Biography rather makes one wish for more. The poem
itself I have not been able to procure. The volume of
the *Lady's Magazine* containing it is not in the British
Museum, and the biographer only tells us that "he

discovered one after a long search." This little triumph, however, seems to have been the turning-point in Crabbe's life. Miss Elmy, whom he now celebrates under the name of Mira, shared his enthusiasm ; and he continued to write verses, "upon every occasion and without occasion," till he had composed enough to fill a large quarto, of which, however, the editor of his poems has very sparingly availed himself. With the year 1774 dates his first serious appearance as a candidate for poetic honours, when he found means to publish at Ipswich his poem on "Inebriety." The piece, though unsuccessful, is something more than a good imitation of Pope. The versification is finished, and some of the descriptions are vividly and even powerfully written. It is curious that he should have introduced into this poem a bitterly satirical portrait of a domestic chaplain—

> "The easy chaplain of an Atheist lord,"

a character of which he knew nothing by experience, and could have learned little from books. Common report, we fear, must have been his only guide ; and, no doubt, village gossip was as busy then as ever with the doings of the nearest great house, which, if less sensational in some other respects, were more boisterous and convivial then than they are in these decorous days. It was at this time also, that wandering about the Suffolk woods with Miss Elmy, he contracted that taste for botany, which was afterwards one of his greatest pleasures, and which he found a great resource when things were not going altogether pleasantly with him at Belvoir Castle.

In the year 1775 Crabbe's apprenticeship expired, and he returned to Aldeburgh, hoping to be able to proceed to London and complete his education at the hospitals. His father, however, was unable to afford the expense, and Crabbe was compelled once more to fall back upon the quay at Slaughden, and busy himself with cheese and butter casks in the dress of a common warehouseman. Here he was found, on one occasion, by one of his Woodbridge friends, who was practising in the neighbourhood, and expressed great indignation at his meekly submitting to such a lot. But what was he to do? The friend who despised him for earning his livelihood in the only way that was open to him should have shown him how to do better before urging him to quit it. Quit it, however, Crabbe did at last, and came to London for a short time to learn what he could of his profession, to which he still looked as the serious business of his life. What made Aldeburgh additionally disagreeable to him at this particular period was the change for the worse in his father, who had now contracted habits of intemperance, which made him the terror of his family. He was still anxious, however, to promote his eldest son's prospects, and sent him to London in 1777, as we must suppose at some considerable sacrifice. He lodged with some Aldeburgh people near Whitechapel for about eight months, till all his money was gone, when he returned to Suffolk, and became assistant to Mr. Maskill, who had lately begun business there as a surgeon and apothecary. It is said that while in London his landlady accused him of body-snatching. "Dr. Crabbe," she affirmed, "had dug up William," a child of her own, which had been recently buried; and he narrowly escaped being carried before the Lord Mayor.

On Mr. Maskill leaving Aldeburgh in 1777, Crabbe set up for himself; but his practice was confined to the poorer classes, who, seeing him botanising among the dykes, came to the conclusion that his medicines were distilled from the roots and herbs which he gathered there, and that what cost him nothing he was bound to dispense gratis. He was now, however, his own master, and could spend as much time as he pleased in the society of Miss Elmy. But his profession continued to frown upon him; nor did the brief increase of practice which attended the quartering at Aldeburgh, first of the Warwickshire, and afterwards of the Norfolk Militia, 1778–9, make much real difference to his prospects. But he enjoyed the society of the officers, and especially of Colonel Conway, who could hardly have been, as the biography represents, the celebrated Field-Marshal Conway, Secretary of State from 1765 to 1768. This gentleman, who had been colonel of the Blues, was now a general, and immersed in politics. The colonel seems to have been much pleased with Crabbe, and presented him with some Latin treatises on botany, amongst them Hudson's *Flora Anglica*, in studying which he greatly improved his knowledge of Latin, and thus enabled himself, not only to pass his examination for holy orders, but also to appreciate Horace.

Whether any of the Militia officers were introduced to Miss Elmy we are not informed; but Crabbe's son tells us that at this time his father was tormented by fits of jealousy. The young lady was pretty and lively, and in such society as she frequented was the object of a good deal of attention. Crabbe probably was no proficient in the graces ; and most of the gentlemen who hung about his intended would probably be his superiors in manner and knowledge of the world. What he suffered under these circumstances may easily be imagined. But it does not appear that any quarrel was the result. Miss Elmy came to stay with Crabbe's parents at Aldeburgh, who soon conceived a strong attachment for her, while Crabbe, in his turn, was a constant visitor at Beccles, at the house of his future mother-in-law. The betrothed couple used to go out fishing together in the river Waveney, and gathering wild flowers in the neighbouring woods ; and, in spite of the uncertainty which hung over their future, these must have been happy days. Crabbe, however, was not formed to look on the bright side of things ; and though he has commemorated his rambles with Mira in some boyish verses of a very conventional type, in none of the poems on which his fame rests does he convey the idea that he had ever been a very happy man. On one of these excursions Crabbe, it is said, had a narrow escape from drowning. He left Miss Elmy seated by the side of the river with her fishing-rod, while he went in search of a suitable spot for bathing. Ignorant of the depth of the river, he plunged boldly into the first inviting looking pool, and was immediately carried off his legs, and only saved by some of the long tough rushes which grow in these sluggish streams, and which enabled him to regain his footing.

Shortly after this he was seized with a severe illness while Miss Elmy was staying at Aldeburgh. She remained with his sister to nurse him, and seems to have caught the fever herself ; for when she

returned to her uncle's house at Parham, she was
so ill that her life was despaired of. Crabbe, who
was invited to stay there at the same time, used
often to describe to his children the anxiety which
he underwent at this period, more especially " the
feelings with which he went into a small garden her
uncle had given her to water her flowers ; intending
after her death to take them to Aldborough, and keep
them for ever."   Miss Elmy recovered her health,
but it was now becoming high time that some effort
should be made by George to place himself in a better
position, or else that the engagement should be aban-
doned.   It is true he was only five-and-twenty ; but the
lady was approaching thirty.   And Crabbe was beginning
to despair of ever succeeding as a surgeon.   Independently of the very imperfect professional education which
was all he had received, he was not fitted by nature
for a calling which demands quickness of apprehension,
promptness of decision, and great manual steadiness
and dexterity.   Crabbe possessed none of these qualities ;
and conscious of possessing others which might lead to
fortune if he could ensure them fair-play, the only wonder
is that he lingered at Aldeburgh so long.   In spite of
pecuniary obstacles, he would probably have found
means to escape had he not been detained by the dread
of parting from Miss Elmy.   But the hour came at
last.   " One gloomy day, towards the close of the year
1779, he had strolled to a bleak and cheerless part of the
cliff above Aldeburgh called the ' Marsh Hill,' brooding
as he went over the humiliating necessities of his
position.   He stopped opposite a muddy, shallow piece
of water, as desolate and gloomy as his own mind,

called the leech-pond ; and it was 'while I gazed on it,'
he said to my brother and me one happy morning, 'that
I made up my mind to go to London and venture all.'"
He had not then heard of the fate of Chatterton, or he
might still have been shaken in his purpose. As
it was, he borrowed five pounds of Mr. Dudley North,
brother to the candidate for Aldeburgh ;* and after taking a tender farewell of Miss Elmy, arrived in London
some time in April 1780, with a box of clothes, a case of
surgical instruments, a bundle of manuscripts, and
three pounds in money.

* At the ensuing general election, September 1780.

CHAPTER II.

I N more respects than one it was fortunate for Crabbe
that he was enabled to leave Aldeburgh. He would
have made, at the best, but an indifferent surgeon ;
and without the patronage which he found in London,
could never have got his poetry before the public.
But this is not all. While an apprentice at
Woodbridge, and afterwards while his own master at
Aldeburgh, he seems to have acquired a taste for conviviality, which even in those bacchanalian days attracted
notice. These tastes were not indulged, I should imagine,
in very choice company, and by his removal to London
he escaped the danger, at all events, of being tempted
into vulgar debauchery.

His only friends in London were a Mr. and Mrs.
Burcham, the latter being a friend of Miss Elmy,
who were established as linen-drapers on Cornhill. To
be near them, Crabbe took lodgings at the house of Mr.
Vickery, a hair-dresser by the Royal Exchange, from whom
he bought a fashionable wig, of which the price made
a serious inroad on his capital. But he did not at first,
it seems, anticipate all the misery that was in store for him.
Among his MSS. were the two poems of the "Village" and

the "Library ; " yet it does not appear that these were among the pieces which he submitted in the first instance to the London publishers. After several short poems had been declined, he at last found a publisher in H. Payne, a bookseller in Pall Mall, for " The Candidate : a Poetical Epistle addressed to the Authors of the *Monthly Review.*" Both the *Monthly Review* and the *Gentleman's Magazine* treated it very coldly, but had not the publisher failed, Crabbe would probably have received a few guineas for his work. Crabbe seems to have been of opinion that the *Monthly Review* was the leading critical journal of the day ; but, according to Dr. Johnson, it was inferior to the *Critical Review ;* and had Crabbe addressed himself to this, he might have experienced a better fate.

" The Candidate " is very unequal to the rest of Crabbe's earlier productions. It is desultory, and the reviewers were right in saying that the author laboured under that "material defect, the want of a subject." Payne's failure was a serious calamity, and in the meantime all other literary efforts were doomed to disappointment. He began a long prose treatise, entitled *A Plan for the Examination of our Moral and Religious Opinions*, which he obtained permission to dedicate to Lord Rochford ; but when he applied to that nobleman for more substantial assistance, his letters were unanswered. How he lived during the first part of his sojourn in London we learn from the journal which he kept for the benefit of Mira (Miss Elmy), a record of hopes, fears, trials, and disappointments more melancholy even than Chatterton's. But how he lived afterwards, when his money had long since been spent, and all his books, instruments, and clothes gradually sold or pawned, it is painful to conjecture. The last entry in the Journal is dated June 11th, and it yet wanted eight months of the time when a helping hand was to be stretched out to him. We must suppose that he received some little assistance from his father, and at Mrs. Burcham's table he was sure of a dinner if he was known to be in want of one. But Crabbe was too proud to accept eleemosynary hospitality. He seems to have earned nothing, and this is all we know. We may picture him to ourselves leading very much the same life as many another candidate for literary fortune had led before him: slinking from his lodgings to the nearest coffee-house for a crust of bread, ashamed of the ragged coat and broken shoe, or roaming about the great city, trying to forget the pangs of hunger when he could not afford even that; waiting eagerly for the answers of publishers, which were always refusals; and looking forward, with that sickening of the heart with which few can sympathise but those who have undergone it, to the period when he must abandon all hopes of literary success, and again become a doctor's drudge.

His life, however, was not one of abject or unmitigated wretchedness. He was able, at his first coming to town, at all events, to spend a few pence once or twice a week at a coffee-house in the city, where he met several young men of ability and information, whose companionship was a great relief to him. Among them his biographer distinguishes three—Mr. Bonycastle, afterwards master of the Military Academy at Woolwich; Mr. Dalby, afterwards Professor of Mathematics at the Military College at Marlow; and a Mr. Burrow, a merchant's clerk, who afterwards rose high in the service of the East India Company. Mr. Bonycastle seems at that time to have been giving lessons in mathematics, and Crabbe frequently accompanied him in his suburban walks. By himself he visited Hampstead Heath and Hornsey, and in Hornsey Wood resumed his botanical researches. He generally carried in his pocket a small edition of some Latin poet; and one summer evening, being too tired to walk home, and unable to pay for a bed at any public-house, he amused himself with Tibullus till it was dark, and then slept upon a haycock till the morning. One who could do this can not have been wholly miserable.

The last we hear of him is during the well-known Gordon riots, of which his journal contains a very graphic picture. But what became of him during the ensuing winter we have no means of ascertaining. He seems to have retained his lodgings at Mr. Vickery's, and it may have been to him that he owed the £14, to which he refers in his letter to Mr. Burke. It appears that he had, according to the fashion of that time, "circulated proposals" for the above-mentioned work on the *Examination of our Moral and Religious Opinions*, and that a certain number of subscriptions had been promised, which he was expecting very shortly to receive. But his creditor, whoever he might be, refused to wait. A debtor's prison stared Crabbe in the face. He had applied in vain to Lord North, Lord Thurlow, and Lord Shelburn, to whom he addressed two poetical epistles; and he often contrasted his receptions at Shelburn's door in Berkeley Square in 1780, with the welcome that awaited him afterwards at

Lansdown House. As a last desperate effort, he wrote the celebrated letter to Burke, the original of which is still preserved at Barton, near Bury St. Edmunds, the seat of the Bunbury family. I cannot quote it at full length, but its most interesting portion runs as follows :—

" SIR,—I am sensible that I need even your talents to apologise for the freedom I now take ; but I have a plea which, however simply urged, will, with a mind like yours, Sir, procure the pardon. I am one of those outcasts on the world who are without a friend, without employment, and without bread. Pardon me a short preface. I had a partial father, who gave me a better education than his broken fortune would have allowed, and a better than was necessary. As he could give me that only, I was designed for the profession of physic ; but not having wherewithal to complete the requisite studies, the design but served to convince me of a parent's affection, and the error it had occasioned. In April last I came to London with three pounds, and flattered myself this would be sufficient to supply me with the common necessaries of life till my abilities should procure me more. Of these I had the highest opinion, and a poetical vanity contributed to my delusion. I knew little of the world, and had read books only. I wrote, and fancied perfection in my compositions ; when I wanted bread they promised me affluence, and soothed me with dreams of reputation, whilst my appearance subjected me to contempt.

"Time, reflection, and want have shewn me my mistake. I see my trifles in that which I think the true light ; and whilst I deem them such, have yet the opinion that holds them superior to the common run of poetical publications."

Here follows an account of his immediate difficulties :—

"You will guess the purpose of so long an introduction. I appeal to you, Sir, as a good, and let me add, a great man. I have no other pretensions to your favour than that I am an unhappy one. It is not easy to support the thoughts of confinement ; and I am coward enough to dread such an end to my suspense.

"Can you, Sir, in any degree, aid me with propriety? Will you ask any demonstrations of my veracity? I have imposed upon myself, but I have been guilty of no other imposition. Let me, if possible, interest your compassion. I know those of rank and fortune are teased with frequent petitions, and are compelled to refuse the request even of those whom they know to be in distress : it is therefore with a distant hope I venture to solicit such a favour ; but you will forgive me, Sir, if you do not think proper to relieve. It is impossible that sentiments like yours can proceed from any but a humane and generous heart.

"I will call upon you, Sir, to-morrow, and if I have not the happiness to obtain *credit* with you, I must submit to my fate. My existence is a pain to myself, and everyone near and dear to me are distressed at my distresses. My convictions, once the source of happiness, now embitter the reverse of my fortune, and I have only to hope a speedy end to a life so unpromisingly begun ; in which (though it ought not to be boasted of) I can reap some consolation from looking to the end of it.

"I am, Sir,
"With the greatest respect, your obedient humble servant,
"GEORGE CRABBE."

The effect of this letter was to raise Crabbe at once from the jaws of ruin to a position of comparative security, and to make it his own fault if he ever wanted a dinner again. The Wickham Brook garret, the Slaughden Quay, the plough, the dung-cart, and the butter casks, the shabby clothes, the scornful jest, all lay far behind him now. Fame and competence, a happy marriage, and an easy life, were within his grasp. The transformation, one may say, was the work of a moment. What Crabbe's feelings must have been at this sudden deliverance from all his troubles, it would need a poet like himself to picture. But we may safely say that rich as are the annals of literature in extraordinary vicissitudes, and in all the romance and pathos of human life, they hardly contain a more

interesting or touching incident than the introduction of
Crabbe to Burke.

Crabbe had enclosed with his letters a packet of MS.
verses, among which were the "Library" and the
"Village," which Burke singled out from the rest as
the work of a real poet ; at once inviting the author
to call upon him. It is said that the first verses
which excited his admiration were those in which Crabbe
describes his own parting from his native place, and
the difference between the rural life imagined by the
poets, and such as it really was upon the coast of Suffolk.
Instead of "the simple life that Nature yields,"

> " Rapine and wrong and fear usurped her place,
> And a bold, artful, greedy savage race.
> As on the neighbouring beach yon swallows stand,
> And wait for favouring winds to leave the land,
> While still for flight the ready wing is spread—
> So waited I the favouring hour, and fled—
> Fled from these shores where guilt and rapine reign,
> And cried, ' Ah ! hapless they who still remain—
> Who still remain to hear the ocean roar,
> Whose greedy waves devour the lessening shore,
> Till some fierce tide,* with more imperious sway,
> Sweeps the low hut and all it holds away.' "

But there are better lines than these in the "Village,"
to say nothing of the fact that the poets have never
sought for Arcadian simplicity and rural innocence in a
maritime town, and among a race of fishermen, so that
the contrast here attempted between the real and the ideal
is misplaced. The poem, on the whole, however, fully
justifies Burke's admiration, and his inclination to assist
the author was not diminished by making his acquaint-

* See page 11.

ance. His son dwells on this fact, as showing that, notwithstanding the roughness and meanness of Crabbe's early life and education, he had a natural good breeding, which to a great extent overcame these disadvantages, though it was long before he quite shook off all the marks of Aldeburgh society, and the "surly savage race" with whom so much of his time had been spent. Burke, however, told Sir Joshua Reynolds, that Crabbe had the mind and feelings of a gentleman ; and after he had satisfied himself by a personal interview, he invited the young man to become an inmate of his house, and charged himself with his future fortunes.

Burke selected, as I have said, the "Library" and the "Village," and pointing out their weak places, recommended the author to set about correcting them at once. When the "Library" had been duly revised, Burke took it himself to Dodsley, to whom Crabbe had previously applied in vain, and read out some passages to the publisher. But even then he declined to publish it at his own risk, and we may suppose that Burke took that upon himself. The poem succeeded, and Dodsley handed over the publisher's profits to the author. This supply of money was very welcome. Crabbe now became acquainted with Johnson, Reynolds, Fox, and other literary and political notabilities, who all took much notice of him. But to frequent society of this kind, entails certain expenses which those that are accustomed to them never think of, and which Crabbe had not the means of meeting. In those days great attention was paid to the article of dress, which was more expensive than it is now. Crabbe was obliged to equip himself with the usual attire of a gentleman, and the small sum which he had received from

Dodsley being soon exhausted, the tradesmen with whom he dealt became troublesome. Of Burke, who had done so much for him, he did not like to ask more. And he was already beginning to feel a return of his former anxieties, when a *Deus ex machinâ* appeared for the second time in the person of Thurlow, the Lord Chancellor. Crabbe had sent his lordship a second poem, when he found he neglected the first, in the form of a personal satire. But the old man bore no malice. He invited Crabbe to breakfast; told him he ought to have noticed his first letter, and that he forgave the second, and at parting gave him a hundred pounds. With part of this money Crabbe relieved several poor scholars with whom a community of poverty had made him intimate, a practice which he is said to have continued for the remainder of his life, as often as he came to London.

Johnson gave him a taste of his "claws," as Gibbon might have said, the first day he met him at dinner, but afterwards received him very kindly at Bolt Court, where he bestowed one piece of advice on him which he ever afterwards remembered—" Never fear putting the strongest and best things you can think of into the mouth of your speaker, whatever may be his condition," though this rather reminds one of Goldsmith's saying, that if the doctor had to make little fishes talk he would make them talk like whales.

Thurlow's invitation seems to have been connected with a conversation between Burke and the young poet soon after they became tolerably well acquainted with each other. When Burke went to Beaconsfield he made Crabbe his companion, and one day, when out for a walk upon the farm, he quoted a passage from the

Georgics with which Crabbe happened to be familiar, and which suggested further conversation on general literature. It may have been then, for the first time, that Burke became aware of Crabbe's classical attainments, which, slight as they were, proved of great value to him at that moment. At the extent of his general information he had early been surprised. "Mr. Crabbe," he said, "seems to know a little of everything." He now began to question him more closely on his past life and future hopes; and when he found that he inclined towards the Church, congratulated him on his Latin, and told him he had reason to be grateful to his father for sending him to his second school. It was then determined that Crabbe should be a clergyman, if a bishop could be found to dispense with a University degree; and Dr. Yonge, Bishop of Norwich, having been prevailed upon, with some difficulty, to make this concession, Crabbe began to prepare diligently for his examination.

It was during this period that the breakfast with Thurlow took place, and the Chancellor, in addition to the bank note, promised to serve him more substantially as soon as he was in holy orders. He continued to be domesticated with Burke while he was reading for ordination, and experienced the same unflagging kindness and consideration to the end. Of this his biographer quotes a trifling instance, which is, however, eloquent enough. One day, when some expected company did not arrive to dinner, the servants kept back a particular dish which had been prepared for them. When Mrs. Burke learned the reason of its absence, she immediately ordered it to be brought up. "Is not Mr. Crabbe here?" she said. Crabbe must have felt some pangs at the prospect of parting from such a patron as this. He was not obliged to leave town as soon as he was ordained deacon, a rite which was performed on the 21st of December 1781, and whether he took any duty or not in London I have not ascertained. But in the following August 1782, being ordained priest in the Cathedral at Norwich, he was licensed curate to Mr. Bennett, the Rector of Aldeburgh, and returned home after an absence of just eighteen months.

He returned victorious. He had proved that he was right, and that his confidence in his own abilities to raise himself above the level of a warehouseman was not misplaced. He had put to shame the prophecies of both friends and enemies. He had left them an outcast and a pauper. He came back famous and prosperous: and of that most delicious of all draughts, that honourable pride which everyone must feel in similar circumstances, he had now his fill. Yet his return home was not, upon the whole, happy. His mother was dead, and Crabbe felt her loss most deeply. His father, it is true, now at last thoroughly believed in him. But it seems that his good fortune excited as much envy as sympathy among his former associates. They circulated spiteful stories at his expense. His evenings at "the Lion" were brought up against him, while, on the contrary, some declared that he had turned Methodist. When he first mounted the Aldeburgh pulpit he saw unfriendly faces looking up at him, and was only too glad when an opportunity offered of exchanging the curacy at Aldeburgh for another situation, which

Burke's interest had secured for him. He had
pressed Miss Elmy to an immediate marriage, but she
had declined till he obtained a living, and seeing the
best promise of one in the position now offered to him,
he, in November 1782, became chaplain to the Duke of
Rutland, and took up his abode at Belvoir Castle.

This was that young Duke of Rutland who took the
side of Mr. Pitt in his struggle with the Coalition, and whose
early death cut short a career of great promise.   He was
the son of the famous Marquis of Granby, the hero of
Minden, and married one of the most beautiful women
in England—Mary Isabella Somerset, daughter of the
fourth Duke of Beaufort.   She and the Duchess of
Devonshire were the two rival beauties of the day, and
keen political opponents.   They lived, I have heard, to
become warm friends afterwards.   Their portraits once
stood side by side in the picture gallery at Belvoir, but
were destroyed in the great fire of 1816.   The Duke
himself, the all-gracious chief of a house in whom gracious-
ness is hereditary, besides being a sportsman and a states-
man, was a man of highly cultivated mind, and fond of
literature and poetry.   He was never better pleased than
when he could escape from the company at the castle
and take a solitary ride with his chaplain, discussing
questions of taste and criticism.   The Duchess herself
was as charming as she was lovely ; and with such a
host and hostess, in such a home as Belvoir Castle,
a poet should have found himself thrice blessed.

The famous castle stands in the north-eastern corner of
Leicestershire, at the end of a long ridge rising abruptly
out of a wide open plain, called by courtesy the Vale of
Belvoir.   The slopes on each side of it are beautifully

wooded, and from the ramparts of the castle seven counties are visible—Lincolnshire, Nottinghamshire, Derbyshire, Warwickshire, Leicestershire, Northampton-shire, and Rutland. On a clear day, on the extreme horizon the eye rests on Lincoln Cathedral, and the spires of Newark and Nottingham seem close at hand. Only one tower of the existing fabric is very ancient, the rest having been built in comparatively modern times. Almost the entire pile, the work of John, fifth Duke, son of Crabbe's early patron, was destroyed by fire in 1816, just as the last finishing touches were being added to it. The Duke was at Newmarket at the time, and the messenger from Belvoir, who had ridden night and day with the news, galloped up to him on the course, exclaiming that the castle was burned to the ground. "Then build it up again," was the Duke's only answer, as he turned back to the business of the day. In this conflagration the apartments inhabited by Crabbe were reduced to ashes. But the rooms allotted to the present chaplain are on the same site, and look out upon the same view which must have greeted Crabbe's eyes the first morning that he opened them at Belvoir.

Had Crabbe been of a different disposition, the Duke and Duchess of Rutland might have been to him all that the Duke and Duchess of Queensberry were to Gay. But neither his natural temperament, nor his early education, qualified him to mingle at his ease in such a circle as he found at Belvoir. He had been soured by disappointment, and his spirits had been crushed by penury. Life had been to him for many years one long and cruel struggle against want, against scorn, against despair. It

was not all at once that he could find any attraction in
the polished gaiety and *insouciance* of high-bred manners,
or endeavour to assume them with success.   Like one
suddenly saved from shipwreck, or rescued from starva-
tion on some desert island, he was not yet attuned to the
common cheerfulness of ordinary society.   During those
early years at Wickham, Aldeburgh, and in London,
his mind received a bias from which it never afterwards
recovered.   His poetry retained to the last the mingled
elements of sadness and bitterness which distinguished it
at first.   No doubt, though softened to some extent by
kindness and success, he brought with him to Belvoir
the frame of mind which he has so well described :—

> " The peevish spirit caused by long delay,
>   When, being gloomy, we contemn the gay."

Add to this, that until he came to live with Burke, he
could have had no experience whatever of the ordinary
usages of society; and though the year that he passed
with his benefactor may have wrought a great improvement in him, it could not have done much to give him
the bearing of a man of the world.   At Burke's he met
only congenial spirits, who were never tired of talking
with him on literature and art.   But at Belvoir Castle he
would find himself in a totally different atmosphere,
listening to conversation on subjects which he did not
understand, and teeming with allusions to a world of
which he knew nothing.   He would meet with only
kindness and civility from all ; and with more than
that from the master and mistress of the castle.   But a
consciousness of his own inability to catch the tone of
the place, or to adapt himself in a moment to its light-

hearted geniality, must have exercised a depressing influence on his manner, and have made him more awkward than he was by nature.

That he did not "get on" thoroughly well in his new position seems admitted on all hands. But there is a passage in the Biography which seems to point to other causes for his failure besides those which I have mentioned. In 1784 the Duke of Rutland was appointed to the Lord-Lieutenancy of Ireland; and Crabbe's son very justly observes that he might naturally have been expected to take Crabbe with him, and provide for him in the Irish Church. This leads him on to consider his father's disqualifications for the position which he held at Belvoir, and would afterwards have held at Dublin, and he admits that Crabbe's manners may still have retained traces of vulgarity, such as he does not scruple to call "repulsive." If this were so, it lends additional significance to the passage we are about to quote, whatever interpretation we are to place upon it, for it seems susceptible of more than one:—" Mr. Crabbe could never conceal his feelings, and he felt strongly. He was not a stoic, and freedom of living was prevalent in almost all large establishments of that period; and when the conversation was interesting, he might not always retire as early as prudence might suggest; nor, perhaps, did he at all times put a bridle to his tongue, for he might feel the riches of his intellect more than the poverty of his station." We suppose we may gather from this and other passages that Crabbe was inclined to be dogmatic, apt to contradict his company with more freedom than discretion, and with more vigour than good breeding. But are we to infer anything more than this? What is the meaning of this reference to "freedom of living?" and to Crabbe's failure to retire "as early as prudence would suggest?" Does it mean that his presence was a restraint upon the party after dinner, and that if he had been a "three-bottle" man like themselves, and able to talk about horses and hounds as well as books, the colour of his cloth, or the quality of his manners, would have signified nothing, and they would gladly have hailed him as a boon companion? This is the construction which has generally been placed on this passage. It is supposed that he was rude and disagreeable, without the one redeeming faculty which in those days was allowed to cover a multitude of sins. Perhaps that is what his son meant; though I confess it seems to me that he may have meant exactly the reverse, and that Crabbe, who had at one time certainly been fond of his glass, may have been indebted to the Duke's port for some of those breaches of good taste by which he is said to have given offence. Under the influence of wine, any bad habits which he had contracted in his early youth would reassert their sway, and though only a chaplain, still it was necessary that he should drink like a gentleman.

It is also to be borne in mind that in these early days Crabbe was not only a Whig, but what we should now call a Radical. He had accustomed himself to believe that the poor were neglected and oppressed; that the rich were hard and selfish; that every aristocrat was a tyrant, and every clergyman a drone. Experience and gratitude must have already begun to teach him to question the truth of these impressions; but they could not be shaken off in a day, and would peep out sometimes, we may be sure, in the warmth of post-prandial disputation. We know, at all events, that he was compelled to drink his glass of salt and water for refusing to join in Tory toasts.

Crabbe's connection with Belvoir derives some additional interest from the fact that he was, I think, the last English man of letters who stood in this kind of relation to the great. It had formerly been common. But the Duke of Rutland was the last of the patrons, in this sense of the word at least; and writers were now beginning to look to the public for support, rather than to the munificence of individuals. In Macaulay's essay on Johnson is to be found the *locus classicus* on this subject, and it may be that Crabbe himself was dimly conscious that he was more or less in a false position. In an earlier generation no suspicion of the kind would have occurred to him. It had once seemed quite natural that poets and artists should be domiciled with nobles and princes; and they conferred as much honour as they received by their presence in the palace or the castle. Then such was the only mode by which the professors of literature, and literature itself, could be supported. But as soon as it became possible for writers to earn a competent income by the sale of their works to the public, so soon did their dependence on patronage come to be regarded as undignified. Crabbe began to write before the transition was completed. Though possible, it was still difficult, for an unknown poet to get his verses before the public without the assistance of some influential sponsor. But Johnson and Goldsmith had shown that it could be done, and the former's letter to Lord Chesterfield gave its death-blow to the old system.

Crabbe, it is true, was the duke's chaplain, and as such had an assured position in the household, which simply

as an author he might not have had. Still it was his
literary merit which had secured him the duke's favour,
and it was rather as a poet than a clergyman that he
claimed the recognition of his patron's guests. He may,
no doubt, have been painfully reminded sometimes that he
was now among men who were unable, not from want of
kindness, but from want of experience, to regard him
with the eyes of Burke and Reynolds, or make the same
allowance either for his dependent situation or his
personal peculiarities. It is gratefully acknowledged by
his son, however, that none of the mortifications which
Crabbe certainly seems to have encountered while a
resident at Belvoir, were in the smallest degree attrib-
utable to the Duke and Duchess of Rutland. He was
treated by them uniformly as he had been treated by
Mr. and Mrs. Burke.

Many years afterwards Crabbe published among his
tales the well-known story of "The Patron," a severe
satire on the noble lord who takes a poor poet into his
household, and, after feeding him for a time with luxury
and flattery, disappoints him so completely in the end that
the unfortunate youth first loses his reason, and then,
on recovering, dies of a broken heart. It should not,
I think, have been left to Crabbe's biographer to explain
that this tale, though strongly coloured by his reminiscences of Belvoir Castle, bore no reference whatever to
the high-minded and generous nobleman who had been
his own patron, and whose widow continued, long after
her husband's death, to be his friend and benefactress.
In the tale of "The Patron," the poet is supposed to
possess some claim upon "Lord Frederick" for political
services rendered to him. But Crabbe had rendered

none to the family of Belvoir, whose regard for his interests, when not prompted by pure kindness of heart, could only have been due to a genuine respect for literature.

In Rogers's *Table Talk* we find a story of Crabbe, at a later period of his life, which it is very difficult to believe. Rogers declares that he was once with the poet at a London dinner party where the Duchess-Dowager of Rutland was one of the company, and that Crabbe's reminiscences of Belvoir were so intolerably painful that it was only after a long struggle he could force himself to address her. The story is opposed to all that I have here written of his later intercourse with the Rutland family, and irreconcilable with the partiality displayed for him by the Duchess Isabella in particular. It is more likely that Rogers characteristically gave this colouring to an incident which is susceptible probably of some very different interpretation.

CHAPTER III.

AMONG the guests at the castle whom Crabbe remembered with the greatest pleasure, were the Duke of Queensbury, a distant cousin of Gay's Duke, the Marquis of Lothian, Watson, Bishop of Llandaff, and Dr. Glynn. But the Duke was his chief friend; and we can picture to ourselves the scene on a hunting morning, when all the sportsmen in their scarlet coats were riding slowly down the hill which leads from the Castle terrace, laughing over the previous night's symposium, and discussing the chances of a run across the vale below, while the Duke made his excuses to the party for not joining them at once, and turned back to meet the black-coated chaplain who was waiting to accompany him to some interesting spot in the neighbourhood. Then they would plunge into the subjects nearest to Crabbe's heart, the true definition of poetry, the beauties of Pope and Dryden, the condition of the modern drama, and the merits of the great actors and actresses of the day, of whom at that time Crabbe had only heard. These were golden moments. But what Crabbe specially enjoyed were the periodical visits to Chevely for the Newmarket Races, and occasional excursions to Croxton Park, where there are some large ponds in which the company used to fish. At these times all ceremony was laid aside, and Crabbe was able to amuse himself in his own way. At Croxton Kyriell, a village about eight miles from Belvoir, there are some picturesque woods, through which he would ramble at his leisure the livelong summer day, collecting beetles and moths while the rest were catching pike and perch, and thinking of the days when he wandered through the woodlands of his native county with a companion by his side whom he now hoped soon to call his own.

These rambles must have taken place in the summer of 1783. For Crabbe did not go to Belvoir till late in the autumn of 1782, and in March 1783 the family came to London for the season, when, the duke's town-house being full, Crabbe was lodged in the rooms lately tenanted by the unfortunate Hackman, the lover of Miss Ray, and murderer of Lord Sandwich. In the autumn of that year he went to Suffolk, and when Parliament met in the following November, returned to London with the duke. On the 14th of June 1783 the duke had not left London, for on that day Pitt dined with him in Arlington Street, and about three weeks afterwards Parliament was prorogued. It must, therefore, have been during the months of July and August 1783 that the fishing parties at Croxton Kyriell took place. The Duke of Rutland went to Ireland as Lord-Lieutenant in February 1784, and the hospitalities at Belvoir ceased.

The year 1783 was an eventful one for England, and also an eventful one for Crabbe. It was the year of the Coalition Ministry, of Pitt's appointment as Prime Min-

ister, and the last triumphant stand made by George III.
against the Revolution families. The Dukes of Rutland
had been Whigs, but never very keen partisans. And
now the young head of the house, who had only just completed his twenty-ninth year, touched, as were hundreds
of other young men at the same time, by the appeal
of their sovereign against the dictation of an exclusive
oligarchy, threw himself heart and soul into the Tory
cause, with abilities, as Mr. Froude says, which, but for
his early death, might have "given him a place in the
history of the empire." * Crabbe, therefore, saw London
at a stirring moment, and at the house of the Duke of
Rutland must have met many of the chief actors in the
drama. But his mind was probably pre-occupied with
his own concerns, and his son records that he never cared
to talk about the people with whom he mingled, or the
scenes which he witnessed at this period of his life.

Between his arrival at Belvoir in the previous autumn,
and his return to London in the following spring, he had
completed and revised "The Village," and he now sent
it, by the hands of Mr. Joshua Reynolds, to Dr. Johnson.
Johnson pronounced it "original, vigorous, and elegant,"
and suggested a few alterations, which Crabbe very readily
adopted, though one of them is rather unintelligible.
For instance, Crabbe had written :—

> " In fairer scenes, where peaceful pleasures spring,
> Tityrus, the pride of Mantuan swains, might sing ;
> But charmed by him, or smitten with his views,
> Shall modern poets court the Mantuan muse ?
> From Truth and Nature shall we widely stray,
> Where Fancy leads, or Virgil led the way ? "

* *English in Ireland*, ii., 395.

Johnson wrote :—

> " On Mincio's banks, in Cæsar's bounteous reign,
>   If Tityrus found the golden age again,
>   Must sleepy bards the flattering dream prolong,
>   Mechanic echoes of the Mantuan song?
>   From Truth and Nature shall we widely stray,
>   Where Virgil, not where Fancy, leads the way?"

Crabbe meant to say that, whether Virgil's pastorals were true to nature or not in his own day, they would be purely fanciful now. But what are we to understand by Johnson's line?—

> " Where Virgil, *not* where Fancy, leads the way."

It must mean that Virgil would lead us away from truth and nature, and that fancy, to which Virgil was a stranger, would bring us back to them, fancy being used to signify our own fancy, not Virgil's, employed in the poetical treatment of modern facts. But this is not what Crabbe meant, nor does it seem to me so much to the purpose as the original. A good deal, of course, depends on the sense in which we use the word fancy. If we use it simply to denote the poetic faculty, then truth and fancy are not at variance, because the most poetical representation should also be the truest. If the province of the poet is to reveal qualities in things not immediately discernible by the ordinary understanding, as, for example, the moral effect produced by various kinds of natural scenery, and to display in appropriate language those subtler sympathies of which we ourselves are only dimly conscious, then his is the greater truth, not the less. Perhaps Johnson used the word in this sense. I hope he did. But Crabbe did not. Crabbe meant by it the art of fiction : the power of abstracting from real life some of its most prominent and obvious characteristics, and combining them with all kinds of meretricious embellishments into a species of puppet-show, affording opportunities for poetical description very likely, but in itself the reverse of poetical. Johnson thought that he had expressed Crabbe's meaning more clearly than Crabbe himself. But here, I think, he was mistaken. Johnson's first two couplets are better than Crabbe's, though I do not see the meaning of the word "sleepy ; " while, if in the time of Virgil, Tityrus found the golden age, it could be no dream, and if it was a dream, there could be no contrast. Both then and now it was equally far removed from nature.

"The Village," published in May 1783, was a brilliant success, and established Crabbe's reputation as a real poet. Two out of the three epithets which Johnson has bestowed upon it exactly describe its merits. It is original—for no one ever thought of painting rural life in these characters before. It is vigorous, as any one may see who chooses to turn over its pages ; and if by elegance, though elegance was not Crabbe's strong point, we mean a skilful choice of words, so arranged as to produce the highest effect of which language is capable on any given topic, this praise can hardly be denied to the description of the parish workhouse and the pauper's funeral.

> " Here on a matted flock, with dust o'erspread,
> The drooping wretch reclines his languid head ;
> For him no hand the cordial cup supplies,
> Nor wipes the tear that stagnates in his eyes ;

No friends with soft discourse his pains beguile,
Or promise hope, till sickness wears a smile."

. . . .

" The village children now their games suspend,
To see the bier that bears their ancient friend,
For he was one in all their idle sport,
And like a monarch ruled their little court ;
The pliant bow he form'd, the flying ball,
The bat, the wicket were his labours all ;
Him now they follow to his grave, and stand,
Silent and sad, and gazing hand in hand ;
While bending low, their eager eyes explore
The mingled relics of the parish poor."—*Parish Poor*.

Sir Walter Scott has quoted these lines in the *Antiquary*
in application to Edie Ochiltree.

The literary world were almost as much startled by
Crabbe as they were afterwards by Wordsworth. His
metre was the orthodox metre. But his thoughts and
ideas were far away from the conventional conceptions
of the age ; and when readers nurtured in the fictions
of Goldsmith, Thomson, and Gray's elegy first saw the
truth in Crabbe's pages, they must have acknowledged
the advent of a new power in literature. Crabbe was
undoubtedly guilty of great and reprehensible exaggeration, but his exaggeration was on the side of reality.
If he wrote with the pen of a satirist, it was in the spirit
of one who had witnessed in person the distress which
he was powerless to relieve, and was righteously indignant
with the childish pictures of rural felicity, which had
diverted men's minds from the sad and sober truth.

During these few summer months Crabbe again
enjoyed the society of Burke and Reynolds, the latter
of whom he regarded with peculiar affection. He
especially admired him for his complete imperturbability,

and was probably still better pleased with the absence of all form and ceremony which characterised Sir Joshua's entertainments. One day he dined there in company with the Duke of Rutland and a small but distinguished company, and the contrast between the homeliness and familiarity with which everything was conducted; and the polished manner and high breeding of the guests, seems to have made a lasting impression on him.

As he was now in holy Orders, he might have been expecting soon to hear something from his old friend, Lord Thurlow; nor was he disappointed. Some time in the summer, Thurlow invited him to dinner, and after telling him that, "By God, he was as like Parson Adams as twelve to a dozen," presented him with the two small livings of Frome St. Quintin and Evershot in Dorsetshire, on which, however, he was not obliged to reside. Crabbe's name had been entered by Bishop Watson in the books of Trinity College, Cambridge, that he might obtain a degree after a certain number of terms without residence. Now, however, as a degree was necessary to enable him to hold his new preferment, he obtained an LL.B. at once from the Archbishop of Canterbury, Dr. Moore. Lord Campbell, in his "Life of Lord Thurlow," has omitted to add that the Chancellor kept the promise which he had made two years before, merely observing that there was no doubt he would have done so, had not Crabbe been provided for in the meantime by the Duke of Rutland.

The acquisition of this small preferment did not at first appear either to Miss Elmy or to Crabbe to justify their immediate marriage, and Crabbe returned from his visit to Suffolk in September 1783 without anything

further being arranged on this subject. During the
ensuing winter, however, the poet felt himself more at
ease in his circumstances, and treated himself occasionally
to the theatres. Here he saw Mrs. Siddons, whom he
regarded with that reverential admiration which this great
actress seems to have had the art of exciting above all
her sisters. He was also highly delighted with Mrs.
Abington and Mrs. Jordan, of whom he loved to talk in
after years. I myself have noticed in very old men who
could remember the English stage when this brilliant
constellation still adorned it, a tendency to speak of these
artists with a kind of rapturous enthusiasm such as they
never displayed in the case of poets, painters, or
musicians. Crabbe was one of these. But the time was
now approaching when he was to take a long farewell of
London, for which it is a question after all if he was not
better qualified than for the country.

At the end of 1783, or the beginning of 1784, the Duke
of Rutland received his appointment as Lord-Lieutenant
of Ireland, and as soon as it was determined that Crabbe
was to be left behind, it became necessary to arrange some
mode of life for him. The two chancellor's livings which
he now held were not enough for him to live upon, and
though, as a matter of course, he would at the first opportunity obtain a good living from the duke, his grace had
no vacant preferment at that moment. The duke
accordingly invited him to make the castle his home till
he should be able to settle him on a benefice; and it was
thought that with his household expenses thus taken off
his hands, and with the means which he already possessed,
he might venture to marry without imprudence.

There are some little errors, or obscurities, in his son's

Life—one which I ought to have noticed before, relating
to the death of Lord Robert Manners, who was mortally
wounded in Rodney's action, April 12th, 1782. Crabbe
is made to relate a scene which occurred at Belvoir
between the date of the action and the arrival of the
news of Lord Robert's death. But Crabbe did not go
to Belvoir till late in the autumn of this year, more than
six months after the great battle in the West Indies.
And now, again, his son tells us that "a few weeks"
before the duke embarked for Ireland, Crabbe hastened
to Suffolk to claim the hand of his betrothed. But they
were married in December, and the duke did not sail
for Ireland till the end of the following February, so that
the few weeks could not well have been much less than
three months.

So ended happily an engagement of eleven years'
duration; and it speaks highly for both parties that there
never seems to have been even a momentary idea on
either side of relinquishing the contract. Crabbe had
not yet completed his twenty-ninth year, while the lady
was in her thirty-fourth. She had waited through her
early youth and womanhood for the love of the poor
surgeon's apprentice, though, pretty and agreeable as she
was, she could hardly have wanted suitors of a higher
grade. But the couple were true to each other, and
many years of great happiness were their reward. There
are frequent allusions in his poetry to the sickness of
hope deferred, the misery of long engagements, and the
disappointment occasioned by repeated failures in the
pursuit of independence. He could only have been
thinking of himself and Miss Elmy when he wrote the
following lines many years afterwards :—

" In vain my anxious lover tried his skill
  To rise in life ; he was dependant still ;
  We met in grief, nor can I paint the fears
  Of those unhappy, troubled, trying years.
  Our fleeting joys, like meteors in the night,
  Shone on our gloom with inauspicious light ;
  And then domestic sorrows, till the mind,
  Worn with distresses, to despair inclined.
  When, being wretched, we incline to hate,
  And censure others in a happier state ;
  Yet loving still, and still compelled to move
  In the sad labyrinth of lingering love.

  My lover still the same dull means pursued,
  Assistant called, but kept in servitude ;
  His spirit wearied in the prime of life,
  By fears and wishes in eternal strife."

This is probably a very true picture of the feelings of both Crabbe and his future wife during the long interval which elapsed between their engagement and their marriage; but, in this instance, the too common consequences did not follow. They were married at Beccles Church by the Rev. Peter Routh—father of the famous President of Magdalen, who died in 1855, in the hundredth year of his age—and they almost immediately took up their residence at Belvoir Castle. This arrangement, however, did not last more than one year. As may easily be believed, the half-imaginary slights and discourtesies which the poet seems to have brooded over while living in the castle as chaplain, were trifles light as air compared with what he experienced from the servants in the duke's absence. They would probably be too well trained to be actually uncivil or impertinent, but they would be careless and inattentive; and, at all events, Mr. and Mrs. Crabbe found their residence at the castle so disagreeable that, after the birth of their first child, who lived only a few hours, Crabbe took the curacy of Stathern, about four miles from Belvoir, and went to live in the Parsonage House. Here he resided for four years, till after the death of the Duke of Rutland in October 1787, when he obtained other preferment.

It was during this, and his last year's residence at Belvoir, that he composed the "Newspaper," a poem which, with the "Library" and the "Village," constitute the first division of his works. The "Newspaper," published in 1785, was favourably reviewed, and considered quite worthy of its author; and it is curious that for the next twenty-two years he never published another line. He wrote a memoir of Lord Robert Manners for the *Annual Register*, and in 1778 contributed a chapter on the natural history of the Vale of Belvoir to Nichols's *Leicestershire*. But of poetry not a syllable appeared between the publication of the "Newspaper," in 1785, and the "Parish Register," in 1807.

The four years spent at Stathern were often described by Crabbe as the four happiest years of his life. He and Mrs. Crabbe had the whole range of the woods round Belvoir Castle and at Croxton Park to roam through at their pleasure; and there were no duty calls to be paid at the castle, thronged with fine gentlemen and ladies. Here, in company with his wife, he could follow his favourite pursuits of botany and entomology, unmoved by the necessity of returning home to a formal and ceremonious banquet, and the conversation of a circle in which he could never feel at ease. We can

imagine him often repeating to himself the passages in
"As You Like It," which describe the freedom of life
in the woods, away from the shackles of etiquette and
the "painted pomp" of courts. Here, truly, Crabbe
had no enemy to fear but wind and rough weather. He
was at ease in his pecuniary circumstances. He had
fame; and was now in the first flush of that happiness
which attends the fruition of a long-tried and virtuous
attachment. A happy home, no doubt, was the little
parsonage at Stathern; and Crabbe was sorry to leave it
even for a more lucrative appointment.

The majority of the country clergy at that time, and
especially in the Midland counties, were sportsmen. Of
the better sort of them a portrait has been painted by
George Eliot, which promises to be immortal. Crabbe
and Mr. Gilfil were contemporaries; and while the one was
out hunting with Sir Jasper Sitwell, or shooting over the
Warwickshire stubbles with the old brown setter, which
came at last to be his only companion, the former
was catching insects, picking wild flowers, and making
notes of the plants and birds indigenous to North
Leicestershire. Mr. Gilfil is almost as real to us as
Crabbe himself; and an imaginary conversation between
the two men might be made both amusing and interesting. Both evidently regarded their profession as it was
customary to regard it a hundred years ago. We must
all remember the noble words of Dr. Johnson on this
subject. He was once offered a living if he chose to
take orders, much as Crabbe was. But when told that a
country clergyman's was an easy life, he replied, "No,
Sir, a country clergyman's is not an easy life; and I do
not envy the country clergyman who makes it an easy

life." But here, as in many other matters, he was in advance of his age. No clergyman in Crabbe's days was thought a bad clergyman for living as Crabbe lived. His duties were regarded as rather social and moral than spiritual. To visit the poor, to relieve the sick, to rebuke idleness and immorality, and to set a reasonably good example himself of temperance, soberness, and chastity, was all that was expected of a model country clergyman in the days before the flood; when the Methodism which had stirred the great deeps in our populous cities had not yet penetrated to the secluded wood-girt villages far away from newspapers or coaches, and not a ripple moved the surface of that old-fashioned rural system which seemed made to last for ever. To this standard Crabbe quite came up; and to the pastoral care which he bestowed upon his little flock, he often added the functions of a doctor also, his medical training being a most valuable addition to his clerical qualifications in the days when country doctors were few and far between, and not worth much when found.

Crabbe, it appears, made some attempts to accommodate himself to the sporting habits of his neighbours. During his residence at Stathern he put himself into one of the large, stiff, velveteen shooting jackets, with gaiters and breeches to match, which may still be seen on elderly gamekeepers, and for a season or two carried a gun; but the same unsteadiness of eye and hand which disqualified him for a surgeon disqualified him also for a shot; and, having made this concession to public opinion, he threw his garments on one side, and reserved his gun for the protection of his kitchen-garden. It does not appear that he made any effort to hunt, and in these early days he could not have afforded a horse capable of crossing the vale, though the pace was not then what it has become since. Coursing disgusted him; nor does it seem that the Croxton Park fish-ponds had any charm for him either. His wife and his village, his bookcase and his garden, his flies and his flowers were all that he required to make life pass agreeably and usefully; and one likes to think of him in this little haven of rest—this little interval of happy calm and sunshine, between the anxieties and privations of past years, and other troubles of a different kind that were to come.

It is scarcely necessary to say that he was not the kind of man to form habits of intimacy with the neighbouring vicars and curates, who rode to hounds, shot partridges, played whist, occasionally danced a quadrille, and thought no evil. These men, moreover, would all be staunch Tories; and both from his habits, his manners, and his opinions, they would probably set Crabbe down as a very queer fellow, with whom it was difficult to get on, and who had some very odd notions in his head about the constitution of society.

In October 1787 occurred the sudden death of the Duke of Rutland, then only in the thirty-fifth year of his age; and the impression which Crabbe made upon the family is shown by the anxiety of the duchess, not only to provide for him, but to keep him in the neighbourhood of the castle. While her grief was still fresh she exerted herself on his behalf, and gave him a letter to Thurlow, begging him to exchange the Dorsetshire livings for two that were vacant in Leicestershire. Crabbe called with the letter on Thurlow, who declared with an oath that he would not do such a thing for any man in England. Thus it became necessary for the duchess herself to try the power of her fascination on him ; and as soon as she arrived in London, she called on the rough old lawyer, whose obduracy seems to have vanished at her presence like the violence of the waves before the face of Thetis. He at once granted her request, and nominated Crabbe to the livings of Muston and West Allington—the former a rectory in Leicestershire, about five miles from Belvoir ; the latter, a vicarage within the borders of Lincolnshire. Saunderson, Bishop of Lincoln, was rector of this parish from 1633 to 1642, and Nichols quotes some very amusing extracts from the diary of another rector of Muston, one Henry Knewstub, who held the living forty years, from 1665 to 1705, and who seems to have been a somewhat unclerical character. Crabbe succeeded the Rev. Francis Bacon, who also held West Allington, and who put the house and garden into the state in which Crabbe found them.

I have already mentioned that in Nichols's *Leicestershire* is to be found a chapter by Crabbe on the Natural History of the Vale of Belvoir, the result of many months of research in the woods of Belvoir and Croxton Park. His history extends all over the animal and vegetable kingdom, and includes shells and fossils. It appears that the kite was then common in the neighbourhood of Belvoir. The pheasants turned up in the duke's woods had not thriven and increased, which is curious, considering the number of wild pheasants to be found there now. The deer still ran wild over the vale, though not in great numbers : and the badger and the otter, though not unknown, seem to have been nearly as scarce there at the end of the last century as they are now.

It was in May 1785 that Crabbe removed from Belvoir to Stathern, and it was on the 25th of February 1789 that he removed from Stathern to Muston. Muston is an ordinary Leicestershire village, with a population of about three hundred, situated in rather an uninteresting part of what is not, upon the whole, a picturesque county. The Vale of Belvoir is very flat, and without that abundance of hedgerow timber which gives to many parts of Leicestershire, Northamptonshire, and Warwickshire the appearance of a large park. There are some fine woods in the neighbourhood, but outside of these the appearance of the country is not only level, but even bare. The village itself, however, stands rather prettily on each side of a brook, spanned by what was once an old stone bridge, but now covered over with a coating of bricks. As you cross the bridge coming from Belvoir, the church and Parsonage are on a rising ground to the right, only separated from the road by the churchyard fence and the wall of the rector's garden. The old house in which Crabbe lived was pulled down before his death, and a new one built in its place, on a less favourable situation, higher up the slope. A hundred years ago the Parsonage stood a little to the north of the east end of the church, the windows looking out upon the church-yard and a flower-garden which bordered it, both running down to the edge of the "winding streamlet, limpid, lingering, slow," which is described in the "Borough." On the opposite side of the stream grow some tall elm trees, inhabited by a family of rooks. To the left of the trees are seen, at a little distance, some cottages and farm-buildings, over which, in the near horizon, rise the lordly towers of Belvoir. In Crabbe's time the Parsonage seems to have been divided from the churchyard by a tall hedge, through which an arch was cut to let in the view of the castle. Some elm trees which stood between the house and the church, and perhaps rather darkened the windows, have been cut down, and most of the ornamental trees in the present garden have been planted since the poet's days. One old tree, a mulberry tree, apparently of great age, alone survives, and may perhaps have seen the days of the Puritans; but it has not found a place in any of the poet's rhymes.

The church, itself a mixture of Early English and Perpendicular, is a good specimen of ecclesiastical architecture, and contains a handsome old oak screen, narrowly rescued from destruction by the present rector, who came to the living as the process of "restoration" was proceeding. The reader may be interested in hearing that the old church music, the violin, the flute, and the bassoon, to which Crabbe listened every Sunday, is coming into fashion again, both in that neighbourhood and elsewhere, the clergy finding that it gives the people an additional interest in the church, and that a good band, after all, is no bad substitute for an ill-taught, slovenly choir.

The present rector, Mr. Furnival, who showed me over the church, very kindly took me into his house, and showed me the only relic of Crabbe still remaining in the village—namely, an iron "brand" with G.C. on it, with which he used to brand his garden tools. He also showed me the Register, with some entries in Crabbe's hand-writing, and the record of his wife's death, whose monument may be seen in the church. In the days of the Commonwealth the Parliamentary Committee visited Muston, and pronounced the then rector to be "no preacher, and scandalous." At Muston "the oldest inhabitant" is a labourer, named Daniel Leighton, an old gentleman bent nearly double, but in other respects hale and vigorous. He is eighty-six years of age, and would have been twelve years old when the poet left Muston. But he remembered "Muster Crabbe." Being asked what he was like, he replied, " Oh, a little stiff man ;" and that was all that could be got out of him as regarded Crabbe's personal appearance. He said that he had gone out beating the bounds with Mr. Crabbe, and that when they came to the boundary stones, instead of some unfortunate boy being bumped against them to make him remember the spot, Crabbe distributed nuts and oranges among the school children, as likely to produce the same effect by more benevolent means. He likewise told me of a curious trait of old-fashioned manners which he remembered to have witnessed. He showed me the spot at the bottom of what was Crabbe's garden, where a bathing-house formerly stood ; to which he had often seen " the ladies of the family "—" real ladies," he took care to tell us—come down to bathe in the tiny brook which is not, at this place, much more than a yard in width.

Here, then, in the spring of 1789, Crabbe pitched his tent. But he had not been there three years and a-half when he was called away to Suffolk by the death of his wife's uncle, Mr. Tovell, of Parham. Tovell, as I have said, was a yeoman of the old school, whom Crabbe has commemorated in the "Widow's Tale." His

style of living was very much the same as that to which
Cobbett looked back in after years with so much regret,
though it was not, one hopes, invariably characterised
by the same prodigious conviviality. Crabbe's son and
biographer remembers when he was not quite five years
old being taken to pay the old gentleman a visit, in
September 1790. His father and mother had driven
from Muston to Parham in an old-fashioned gig, with
the boy between them, and occupied three days on the
journey.

"I was then introduced," he says, "to a set of manners and
customs, of which there remains perhaps no counterpart at the
present day. My great-uncle's establishment was that of the first-
rate yeoman of that period—the yeoman that already began to be
styled, by courtesy, an esquire. Mr. Tovell might possess an
estate of some eight hundred pounds per annum, a portion of
which he himself cultivated. His house was large, and the surrounding moat, the rookery, the ancient dove-cot, and the well-
stored fish-ponds were such as might have suited a gentleman's seat
of some consequence; but one side of the house immediately
overlooked a farm-yard, full of all sorts of domestic animals, and
the scene of constant bustle and noise. On entering the house
there was nothing, at first sight, to remind one of the farm: a
spacious hall, paved with black and white marble, at one extremity
a very handsome drawing-room, and at the other a fine old stair-
case of black oak, polished till it was as slippery as ice, and having
a chime-clock and a barrel-organ on its landing-places. But this
drawing-room, a corresponding dining-parlour, and a handsome
sleeping apartment upstairs, were all *tabooed* ground, and made use
of on great and solemn occasions only, such as rent-days, and an
occasional visit, with which Mr. Tovell was honoured, by a neighbouring peer. At all other times the family and their visitors lived
entirely in the old-fashioned kitchen along with their servants. On
ordinary days the family dined in this wise—the heads seated in the
kitchen at an old table; the farm men standing in the adjoining
scullery, door open; the female servants at a side table, called a

bouter ; at the table, perchance some travelling rat-catcher, or tinker, or farrier, or an occasional gardener in his shirt sleeves, his face probably streaming with perspiration.·

"When the dinner was over, the fire replenished, the kitchen sanded and lightly swept over in waves, mistress and maids, taking off their shoes, retired to their chambers for a nap of one hour to the minute.   The dogs and cats commenced their siesta by the fire. Mr. Tovell dozed in his chair, and no noise was heard, except the monotonous cooing of a turtle-dove, varied, however, by the shrill treble of a canary.   After the hour had expired, the active part of the family were on the alert, the bottle (Mr. Tovell's tea equipage) placed on the table ; and, as if by instinct, some old acquaintance would glide in for the evening's carousal, and then another and another.   If four or five arrived, the punch-bowl was taken down, and emptied, and filled again."

Whether Crabbe was much more at home in this kind of society than he had been among the fox-hunters at Belvoir, may reasonably be doubted.   But he had this advantage, that at Parham now, at all events, he was an honoured guest, to whom even the master of the house would be inclined in some respects to look up.   From Parham the Crabbe family went on to Beccles, and from thence to Normanton, where there was a kind of Protestant nunnery established, though apparently on very easy terms.   The abbess herself married Admiral Graves, and another of the sisterhood, Miss Waldron, Crabbe's especial favourite, took her glass and sang her song like one of "the monks of old."   She was especially great in "Toby Philpot."   In the morning she used to drive Crabbe about in her carriage, the poet, it is said, being greatly ·struck with the strength of her understanding and the charm of her conversation.   One Sunday evening at Lowestofft, he was taken to the Dissenting chapel to hear Wesley preach.   He was

introduced to him after the service, and was much
interested by his manners and appearance.

I must now revert to Mr. Tovell's death, which
occurred two years afterwards, in October 1792, and
occasioned a great change in Crabbe's circumstances.
Crabbe was his executor, and his mother-in-law, Mrs.
Elmy, one of his co-heiresses. After a hasty visit
to Parham, as soon as he was summoned, Crabbe
returned to Muston with the determination of placing a
curate in his own parish, and taking up his residence
in Suffolk. This determination was carried out in the
following November, and for thirteen years Crabbe
continued to be an absentee, residing part of the time at
Parham, part at Glemham, and part at a village named
Rendham. These villages lie in a pretty part of the
county of Suffolk, very different from the vale of Belvoir,
and the scenery is, of course, reflected in Crabbe's pages,
especially in the "Lover's Journey," one of the "Tales
in Verse." Great and Little Glemham belonged originally
to a family of the same name, who ruined themselves in
the cause of Charles I. They held on to the property,
however, though they were unable to live there, till
the reign of Anne, when the last of them died in Spain,
without issue, and the estate was sold to Dudley North,
the father of Crabbe's friend. His own seat was at
Little Glemham, and, in 1796, Great Glemham Hall, which
also belonged to him, becoming vacant, it was let to
Crabbe at a low rent, and there he continued to live till
the year 1801, when Glemham being sold, the family
removed to Rendham.

While living at Parham—Parham Lodge it should be
called, I believe—Crabbe took the curacies of Sweffling

and Great Glemham, the former being a benefice in the occupation of the Rev. Richard Turner, the Vicar of Yarmouth; and he here settled down to much the same kind of life as he had led at Muston. He was very glad, however, when the time came for leaving Parham. He did not get on very well with old Miss Tovell, who was one of her brother's co-heiresses, and the evening frequenters of the kitchen missed their accustomed punch-bowl. Crabbe had not the tact to make these changes without giving offence. One of the old *habitués*, the parish overseer, endeavoured to revenge himself by doubling Crabbe's poor-rate, and stated openly his reasons for doing so. The death, at Parham, of Crabbe's third son, by which Mrs. Crabbe's health and spirits were seriously affected, was an additional reason for changing his residence at the first convenient opportunity.

Glemham is described as follows by the author of the Biography, whose boyhood was passed there, and who always remembered it with fondness :—

"A small, well-wooded park occupied the whole mouth of the glen, whence, doubtless, the name of the village was derived. In the lowest ground stood the commodious mansion; the approach wound down through a plantation on the eminence in front. The opposite hill rose at the back of it, rich and varied with trees and shrubs scattered irregularly. Under this southern hill ran a brook, and on the banks above it were spots of great natural beauty, crowned by white-thorn and oak. Here the purple scented violet perfumed the air, and in one place coloured the ground. On the left of the front, in the narrower portion of the glen, was the village; the right, a confined view of richly-wooded fields. In fact, the whole parish and neighbourhood resemble a combination of groves, interspersed with fields cultivated like gardens, and intersected with those green dry lanes which tempt the walker in all weathers, especially in the evenings, when in the short grass of the dry sandy banks lies every few yards a glow-worm, and the nightingales are pouring forth their melody in every direction."

Of Crabbe's ordinary life at this period (1785–1810), we may easily work in the details. He collected flowers and insects in the Glemham woods, and on the neighbouring heaths. He explored the sea-beach for shells and fossils. He took his wife and children for long drives in the one-horse family phaeton, through shady lanes rising between high banks, fragrant with the dog-rose and the honey-suckle, stopping every now and then to gather a specimen, or perhaps to chase a rare butterfly. In the summer evenings, he and his sons either worked together in the garden or strolled about the fields till moonlight, sometimes reading out a novel, and sometimes picking up a glow-worm, the whole party returning to supper amid a concert of nightingales, which then, as now, were abundant in that part of the country. On wet days he occupied himself with his collection, or worked actively at his desk, for though he published nothing, he continued to write incessantly. He now nearly finished an essay on Botany, which he had begun at Muston, and which he offered to Dodsley for publication ; but before it was ready for the press, Crabbe consulted Mr. Davies, vice-Principal of Trinity, Cambridge, who assured him that a scientific treatise on such a subject as botany could not properly be presented to the world in English. Crabbe deferred to his superior judgment on such a point, and burned his essay. But had it been published he would have enjoyed the reputation of a discoverer, as he was the first, it is said, to add to our British flora the

Trifolium suffocatum. It is, perhaps, little known that Crabbe also wrote three novels, of which we may reasonably presume that the characters would be vigorously drawn ; but the plots were suspected to be failures, owing to his want of method and power of selection and combination. These too were burned without being submitted to any other eye but his own.

For society in Suffolk, Crabbe had Dudley North at Little Glemham, who kept him well supplied with fruit and game before he came to Glemham Hall, and Mr. Long, his brother. Mr. Turner, of Yarmouth, was also occasionally his guest ; but Crabbe did not cultivate general society, nor was his wife's health equal to it. At North's house he often met very good society, with whom he would talk over his old London days ; among others Charles Fox, Lord Grey, and Dr. Parr. Fox one day, in passing into the dining-room, pushed Crabbe in front, saying that if he had his deserts he would go before them all. Fox reproached him with his literary inactivity, and promised to revise the next poem he should write ; and soon afterwards we find that he began to try his hand again at poetical composition. By the year 1799, in fact, he had completed a volume of Tales, but on showing them to Mr. Turner, on whose taste he had implicit reliance, that gentleman recommended him to revise them, and Crabbe, taking this to be a polite way of condemning them, threw them in the fire, and set to work upon " The Parish Register," which appeared eight years afterwards.

CHAPTER IV.

ABOUT this time a general complaint began to be heard throughout the country on the subject of non-resident incumbents; and the Bishops thought it necessary to exert themselves to check or put an end to the practice. Bishop Prettyman, the Bishop of Lincoln, now represented to Crabbe that it was his duty to reside at Muston; and although Mr. North endeavoured to procure a remission of the sentence, it was all in vain; and in October 1805, he and his family bade adieu to the woods, the commons, and the waves which they loved so well, and by the end of the month found themselves once more in Leicestershire, settled, as it seemed, for life. Crabbe, however, had not come back to the same Muston which he had left thirteen years before—a quiet agricultural village, reposing peacefully under the shadow of established institutions, and regarding no other authority than that of "the Duke and the Rector," with King George, perhaps, dimly in the back-ground. Between 1792 and 1805 many things had happened. The French Revolution, even where its deeds and doctrines were unknown, had unsettled the minds of the people, who were vaguely aware that some great insurrection had occurred against all they had been accustomed to venerate. In by far the larger number of cases the intelligence only bred disgust, and intensified the old hatred of the French which still possessed the English people. But among certain classes, and in certain parts of the country, it had a different effect, and its influence was very visible in the stimulus which it imparted to Dissent. Accordingly, when Crabbe returned to Muston, he found a Wesleyan congregation established in the parish, and though, as was shewn afterwards by his behaviour to the Dissenters at Trowbridge, he was indifferent to the theological questions at issue between the church and nonconformity, he was irritated by its intrusion into Muston. He always reproached himself with contributory negligence, believing that if a resident clergyman had remained upon the spot this would not have happened. Even as he left Muston, in the autumn of 1792, he had his misgivings, and now he found them more than justified. His own ideas of his spiritual authority were enhanced, perhaps, by the lowness of his origin ; and he seems to have thought it his duty to endeavour to drive out the intruder by violent attacks on him from the pulpit.

This, of course, was the very worst method he could have adopted, only fanning the flame which it was intended to extinguish. But in justice to Crabbe, it must be pointed out that the chief object of his indignation was not the ordinary Wesleyan Chapel, but the assemblies of Calvinistic Methodists, of whom the leader was William Huntington, formerly a day-labourer in Kent, whose works were published in twenty volumes in 1820. Of one of the tracts contained in it, Southey says, "there is nothing like it in the whole bibliotheca of knavery and fanaticism." Of the Huntingtonians, Crabbe himself says:—

" I have only to observe that their tenets remain the same, and have still the former effect on the minds of the converted. There is yet their imagined contention with the powers of darkness, that is at once so lamentable and so ludicrous. There is the same offensive familiarity with the Deity, with a full trust and confidence both in the immediate efficacy of their miserably-delivered supplications, and in the reality of numberless small miracles wrought at their request, and for their convenience. There still exists that delusion by which some of the most common diseases of the body are regarded as proofs of the malignity of Satan contending for dominion over the soul; and there still remains the same wretched jargon, composed of scriptural language, debased by vulgar expressions, which has a kind of mystic influence on the minds of the ignorant. It will be recollected that it is the abuse of those scriptural terms which I conceive to be improper. They are, doubtless, most significant and efficacious when used with propriety, but it is painful to the mind of a soberly devout person, when he hears every rise and fall of the animal spirits, every whim and notion of enthusiastic ignorance, expressed in the venerable language of the apostles and evangelists."

We have only to read Southey's account of William Huntington, to see that whatever indignation Crabbe may have exhibited against his followers, though doubtless injudicious, was nevertheless abundantly justified.

Again, to refer to an author of whom the student of Crabbe is perpetually reminded, do we not see in this passage the identical grievance of Joshua Rann, the parish clerk of Hayslope, when he complained to the Rector that Will Maskery and the Dissenters used Bibles words for their own everyday occasions?

" 'Yes, sir ; but it turns a man's stomach t' hear the Scripture misused i' that way. I know as much o' the words o' the Bible as he does, an' could say the Psalms right through i' my sleep if you was to pinch me ; but I know better nor to take 'em to say my own say wi'. I might as well take the sacrament-cup home, and use it at meals.' 'That is a very sensible remark of yours, Joshua,' said the Rector. ' But as to people saying a few idle words about us, we must not mind that any more than the old church-steeple minds the rooks cawing about it. Will Maskery comes to church every Sunday afternoon, and does his wheelwright's business steadily in the week-days ; and as long as he does that, he must be let alone.' "

The Rector's answer is admirable ; but, unluckily, neither Crabbe's mind nor manners had the repose of Vere de Vere, and he could not help showing his annoyance. We are probably indebted to it, however, for some of the finest verses which Crabbe ever wrote. There cannot be a doubt that the fourth letter in "The Borough," on "Sects and Professions in Religion," was inspired by the wish to scourge the Muston Ranters. But it was necessary to his plan to transfer them to Aldeburgh, and to complete the picture it was requisite to introduce the Roman Catholics. But for the pleasure, therefore, of satirising the Huntingtonians, we should never, perhaps, have had the well-known beautiful lines on the ancient church :—

> " Great was her pride, indeed, in ancient times,
>   Yet shall we think of nothing but her crimes ?
>   Exalted high above all earthly things,
>   She placed her foot upon the necks of kings ;
>   But some have deeply since avenged the crown,
>   And thrown her glory and her honours down ;
>   Nor neck nor ear can she of kings command,
>   Nor place a foot upon her own fair land.
>   Among her sons with us a quiet few,

Obscure themselves, her ancient state review,
And fond and melancholy glances cast
On power insulted and on triumph past :
They look, they can but look, with many a sigh,
On sacred buildings doomed in dust to lie ;
' Of seats,' they tell, ' where priests mid tapers dim,
Breathed the warm prayer, or tuned the midnight hymn ;
Where trembling penitents their guilt confess'd ;
Where want had succour, and contrition rest ;
There weary men from trouble found relief,
There men in sorrow found repose from grief.
To scenes like these the fainting soul retired ;
Revenge and anger in these cells expired ;
By pity soothed, remorse lost half her fears,
And softened pride dropp'd penitential tears.'

Now all is lost ; the earth where abbeys stood
Is layman's land, the glebe, the stream, the wood.
Such is the change they mourn, but they restrain
The rage of grief, and silently complain."

The contrast here raised between the uncomplaining
dignity of the Roman sect and the blatant vulgarity of
all others, was not, perhaps, intended by Crabbe to be
quite so sharp as he has made it. But the sympathetic
tone with which so zealous a Protestant as Crabbe writes
of "our mother church," can only be accounted for by
the fact that he belonged to that party who espoused
the cause of the Roman Catholics, and was thus led to
regard them with a more lenient eye than he would
otherwise have bestowed on them.

During the two years that followed his return to
Muston, Crabbe was busy with "The Parish Register,"
and when it was completed he sent the MS. to Fox.
Here, again, there is some error of chronology in his son's
narrative. If the poem was only completed in the latter

part of the year 1806, it could not have been revised by Fox, as the biographer says it was, for Fox died in July 1806. The poem was probably finished in the spring of 1806, sent to Fox about May, and returned to the author immediately, with Fox's suggestions and criticisms, all which were carefully observed. The poem was published, together with his three previous pieces, and three new ones, " The Birth of Flattery," "Sir Eustace Grey," and the " Hall of Justice," in the following year, the preface to the collection being dated Muston, September 1807. The volumes were dedicated to Lord Holland, and accompanied by a preface, in which the writer offers some excuses for the long interval which intervened between the " Newspaper " and the " Parish Register." But we have seen that though he published nothing, he wrote a great deal, and had he simply said that he wrote nothing to satisfy himself, that would have been sufficient explanation. It is difficult to believe that he was interrupted seriously by the duties of his profession.

The appearance of the "Parish Register" was to Crabbe almost the beginning of a new career. It was universally allowed to possess more than all the merit of his earlier poems ; and he now had on his side the powerful advocacy of the *Edinburgh Review*. As the Review was only begun in 1802, this was the first opportunity of noticing Crabbe which Jeffrey had enjoyed, and his favourable criticism, which will be considered more at length hereafter, sold off the whole of the first edition two days after the article appeared. Fresh editions were called for in 1808, in 1809, and in 1812. By the end of 1809, of which year he spent the autumn and winter at

Aldeburgh, Crabbe had completed the "Borough," which was dedicated to the Duchess of Rutland, and published by Hatchard in 1810. It was pronounced superior to the "Parish Register;" and, in 1812, he followed it up by the "Tales in Verse," dedicated to the Duchess-Dowager, and declared by Jeffrey to be superior to either, and then he gave his pen another long rest for seven years.

During his second residence at Muston, Crabbe seems to have mingled in society more than at any previous period of his life. He often dined at the castle, where he once met Beau Brummel, with whom he was greatly pleased; and also at Sir William Welby's, of Harlaston; at Sir Robert Heron's; with Dr. Gordon Dean of Lincoln, who held the adjoining living; and with several of the neighbouring clergy. But he entertained very little in return, not from any want of hospitality, but because, as his son says, "when the master of the house is a poet, and the mistress always in ill-health, these things will not be done just as they ought to be." Crabbe saw this, and shrank from giving the large dinner parties, with which alone country neighbours entertained each other in the days when luncheon and garden parties were unknown. If we want to know what these dinner parties were like, we have only to turn to Jane Austen, who will tell us all about them in her own softly humorous and delicately graphic style. Another entertainment characteristic of the age was the Assembly Room at Grantham, to which the neighbouring families repaired once a-week for cards and dancing, a fashion that survived almost down to the introduction of railways, which are answerable for the destruction of a good deal of that old rural sociability of which Miss Austen is the painter *par excellence.* Crabbe had long since given up shooting; but he liked his sons to shoot, and was pleased when they made a good bag. So, too, though he had never danced himself, he encouraged his sons to dance, which was then considered quite becoming in a clergyman—witness that model young parson, the Rev. Henry Tilney, in *Northanger Abbey*.

Both the young men had now curacies in the neighbourhood, but still lived at home at Muston. Their mornings and evenings were spent in the old manner. Crabbe still continued his habit of reading aloud; and when the book was a novel, the younger son used to design illustrations for it with a pencil as they went along. In the morning, between breakfast and dinner, he wrote a page, perhaps, of the "Borough" or the "Tales," and in the afternoon, when his parish had no calls upon him, there was the walk or the drive in quest of natural curiosities, or to call on some hospitable neighbour. It does not seem as if angling were one of the family amusements, or else the little stream which ran at the bottom of his garden, and which is dignified in the county histories by the name of the river Devon, afforded excellent perch and gudgeon, which our ancestors had the good taste to consider a delicacy. The present Rector informed me that his children caught them in abundance.

John Crabbe, who was ordained in 1808, was, during part of the second residence at Muston, an undergraduate at Caius College, Cambridge, and there his father went two or three times to visit him. On one occasion John drove his father to Newmarket in a tandem, an excursion which he is said to have enjoyed exceedingly: the odd part of it being, not that Crabbe enjoyed it, but that the son of a country clergyman, not too well off, should have been driving tandems almost as a matter of course, and without incurring any reproach. University manners have, indeed, been wholly revolutionised since the days of Reginald Dalton and Tom Thorpe. Crabbe, how-ever, was now fairly well off. He had in some respects what Swift coveted—six hundred pounds a-year, a river at his garden end, and a comfortable, if not a handsome, house to lodge a friend. His wife had her share of old Mr. Tovell's property. Crabbe's two livings were worth four hundred pounds a-year; and in reckoning up his income, in a letter to Walter Scott, a few years later, he puts it at the above amount, exclusive of what he received from his publisher, which must have formed a substantial addition to it.

The publication of the "Register" brought Crabbe letters from numerous distinguished people: among others, from Lord Grey, Mr. Canning, and Lord Holland, and, perhaps, what he prized still more, one from Mrs. Burke, at Beaconsfield. In 1809 he sent a copy of the third edition to Scott, who answered in a letter dated Ashiestiel, October 21st, 1809, which laid the foundation of their future intimacy. Scott had long been a great admirer of Crabbe, and, like Newman, the poetry which he had loved in his youth, he continued to love in his old age. Only a week before his death he desired to have "a bit of Crabbe" read aloud to him. He was, in 1809, however, in the prime of life, and in the full enjoyment of his own reputation as a poet, though unconscious as yet of the still greater glory that awaited him. In another letter he tells Crabbe with what delight he had read extracts from his earlier poems in 1785, especially the concluding lines of "The Newpaper," warning the poetic aspirant against indulging in unprofitable dreams, and how hardly he could help crying out as he went along, " Why, the man means me ! "

With the publication of *Tales in Verse* in 1812, Crabbe's second period of poetic activity comes to a close, and nearly coincides with other great changes in his life. The *Tales* also were sent to Scott, who this time replied at much greater length. It is interesting to observe the ruling passion coming uppermost at every opportunity. Scott likens Crabbe's position in the Vale of Belvoir, under " the protection of the Rutland family," to his own position at Abbotsford, under the wing of the bold Buccleuch. He is misled, as many others have been both before and after, by the word " vale," by which he evidently understood some well-watered picturesque valley, encompassed by thickly-wooded hills. Crabbe's reply is worth quoting :—

"With respect to my delightful situation in the Vale of Belvoir, and under the very shade of the Castle, I will not say that your imagination has created its beauties, but I must confess it has enlarged and adorned them. The Vale of Belvoir is flat and unwooded, and, save that an artificial straight-lined piece of water, and one or two small streams intersect it, there is no other variety than is made by the different crops—wheat, barley, beans. The Castle, however, is a noble place, and stands on one entire hill, taking up its whole surface, and has a fine appearance from the window of my parsonage, at which I now sit, at about a mile and a half distance. The Duke also is a duke-like man, and the Duchess a very excellent lady. They have great possessions and great patronages, *but*—you see this unlucky particle, in one or other of Horne Tooke's senses, will occur—*but* I am now of the *old race*. And, what then? Well, I will explain. Thirty years since I was taken to Belvoir by its late possessor as a domestic chaplain. I read the service on a Sunday, and fared sumptuously every day. At that time, the Chancellor, Lord Thurlow, gave me a rectory in Dorsetshire, small, but a living ; this the Duke taught me to disregard as a provision, and promised better things. While I lived with him on this pleasant footing, I observed many persons in the neighbourhood who came occasionally to dine, and were civilly received. ' How do you do, Dr. Smith ? How is Mrs. Smith ? ' 'I thank your Grace, well ; ' and so they took their venison and claret. ' Who are these ? ' said I to a young friend of the Duke's. ' Men of the *old race*, sir ; people whom the *old Duke* was in the habit of seeing—for some of them he had done something, and had he yet lived all would have had their chance. They now make room for us, but keep a sort of connection.' The son of the old Duke of that day and I were of an age to a week ; and, with the wisdom of a young man, I looked distantly on his death and my own. I went into Suffolk and married, with decent views, and prospects of views more enlarging. His Grace went into Ireland—and died. Mrs. Crabbe and I philosophised as well as we could ; and after some three or four years, Lord Thurlow, once more, at the request of the Duchess-Dowager, gave me the Crown livings I now hold, on my resignation of that in Dorsetshire. They were at that time worth about £70 or £80 a-year more than that, and now bring me about £400, but a long minority ensued—new connections were formed ; and when, some few years since, I came back into this country and expressed a desire of inscribing my verses to the Duke, I obtained leave indeed, but I almost repented the attempt from the coldness of the reply. Yet, recollecting that great men are beset by applicants of all kinds, I acquitted the Duke of injustice, and determined to withdraw myself as one of the *old race*, and give way to stronger candidates for notice."

Crabbe did the Duke of Rutland some injustice, as we shall see ; nor ought he to have been annoyed at the tone of the Duke's answer, when he begged permission to dedicate the "Borough" to him. The Duke knew nothing of Crabbe personally. When the family went to Ireland he was only twelve years old. When Crabbe left

Leicestershire he was only seventeen. A long interval had elapsed, during which it is very likely that the Duke had scarcely heard his name mentioned. He was a young man, devoted to field sports, and living within a circle not very likely to recall Crabbe to his mind. But we see that although his reply to Crabbe's letter might be less cordial than the Poet had expected, he was not deficient in real kindness. Crabbe was a frequent guest at the Castle, and the Duke finally presented him to the living of Trowbridge, in Wiltshire, and to that of Croxton Kyriel, in Leicestershire, with which he was allowed to hold it, the two together being much more valuable than Muston.

In the summer of 1813, Crabbe and his wife spent three months in London. Mrs. Crabbe was now in very failing health, and the journey was undertaken partly for the sake of gratifying an invalid whim. Crabbe found the principal theatres closed. But the Lyceum was then a minor theatre, and there he saw Liston, who delighted him. His old friend Dudley North also called upon him, and with this gentleman he frequently dined. But of all the old acquaintances whom he met on this occasion the most interesting must have been Mr. Bonycastle, whom he had known in his days of despair, and had never since seen. Exactly one generation had passed since they trod the streets of London, or took their long suburban walks together, Bonycastle working hard for very little, and Crabbe on the verge of destitution. They now met again after this long interval, healthy, prosperous, and famous. What reminiscences they must have revelled in—*Quæ bella exhausta canebant*—the imagination of my readers may conceive as well as mine.

Shortly after Crabbe's return to Muston occurred an event which made a considerable change in his habits and pursuits. On the 21st of October 1813 he lost his wife, after a union of nearly thirty years, which, but for Mrs. Crabbe's continued ill-health and very uneven spirits, would have been one, apparently, of unbroken happiness.* She died in her sixty-third year, and was buried in the chancel of Muston Church, where a tablet marks her resting-place. Crabbe was deeply affected by her death ; and immediately afterwards was seized with a severe illness, by which for some time his life was in danger. Soon after his recovery he received from the Duke of Rutland the welcome offer of the living of Trow-bridge, in Wiltshire, to which he was inducted on the 14th of June 1814 ; and a fresh chapter in his life opens.

It may be proper, at this stage of his career, to say something of Crabbe's political views, which were at one time of rather an extreme character. It is evident that when tramping about the sea-shore at Alde-burgh, or visiting the agricultural labourers in the neighbouring villages after he had begun to practice physic, Crabbe was, as I have said, what we should now call a Radical. But with him, as with many others, a little experience of the society which he had fancied in his ignorance to be corrupt, selfish, and oppressive, wrought by degrees a change in his opinions. After a year and a half spent under Burke's roof, he began to own that in many things he had been mistaken, and that the English aristocracy had their fair share of good qualities,

* " What a father you have ! " Mrs. Crabbe used to say to her sons, when grateful for any one of the innumerable acts of kindness which he was always showing her.

like every other class in the community. It is possible
that, in some respects, his experience of Belvoir Castle
rather revived in him the bitter thoughts which he had
nourished at Aldeburgh, and that he was as fully prepared
as he would have been at any earlier period to welcome
the Revolution when it came. He too, like multitudes of
others, fancied he saw in it the emancipation of mankind from the thraldom of religious and political supersti-
tion. Neither he nor they saw what Burke saw, that it
was at bottom the abnegation of authority, for which we
were all destined to pay pretty dearly in the future. Since
that time, as Newman says of Liberalism, " Phaeton has
got into the chariot of the sun ; the lands which he is
passing over suffer from his driving." Crabbe, however,
no doubt believed that in some round-about way the
French Revolution was to put an end to the parish workhouse and the stinted meal, and the various miseries of
those " poor laborious natives " of whom he had seen so
much, and he welcomed it accordingly. He was one of
those who believed that our first war with France was, in
principle, a war against the spirit of improvement and
reform which only the crimes of the French aristocracy
themselves had clothed with terror ; and not all the
declamation of his friend Burke, to which, by-the-bye, we
scarcely detect a single allusion in Crabbe's life or
writings, ever seems to have reconciled him to it. When
the natural end came, and freedom took refuge in
despotism, which in turn leaned on conquest, Crabbe's
eyes were opened. But meantime he had been accused
of being a Jacobin; and his supposed sympathy with what
were called " French principles " seems to have robbed
him at Muston of whatever popularity he might other-

wise have won by his vigorous denunciation of the "Methodies." But before he died, Crabbe's opinions had advanced much nearer to those of his friend, Sir Walter Scott. Want made him a Radical; society made him a Whig; events made him a Tory. But his conduct was still determined rather by personal feeling than political conviction. At the general election of 1826 he was Croker's proposer at Aldeburgh, and at the same time was nearly torn in pieces by a Tory mob for supporting the Whig candidate in Wiltshire.

Crabbe left Muston some time in the spring of 1814; and on such unhappy terms had he latterly lived with his parishioners that the church bells were rung at his departure.

CHAPTER V.

CRABBE, as we have seen, was inducted to the living of Trowbridge on the 14th of June 1814. He had only just recovered from a severe fit of illness, and the loss of his wife still preyed deeply on his mind. But amid new scenes he gradually recovered his strength and his cheerfulness; and he was soon able to indulge more freely his taste for society, which the state of Mrs. Crabbe's health had latterly prevented him from enjoying. By the principal people at Trowbridge he was very hospitably received. But he seems not to have been much more popular at first than he was in Leicestershire. His predecessor had been an absentee, and his curate was what was called in those days "an awakening man." On the death of the Rector the inhabitants petitioned the duke to give him the living; and the refusal of their request did not incline them to take a more favourable view of the man on whom it was conferred. Crabbe, moreover, here probably, as at Muston, fell to the ground between two stools. He had not the tastes and habits of the old high-and-dry country clergy, nor was he an orthodox Tory. He had not the zeal, the enthusiasm, nor the sanctimony of the Low Church party, whom he shocked by going to balls, plays, and concerts.

With his poorer parishioners he was always too much of the schoolmaster, accompanying his charities with long lectures on the vice or improvidence which made them necessary. But notwithstanding the severity with which he attacked the Dissenters at Muston, his son tells us that at Trowbridge he was singularly liberal in his intercourse with them: and notwithstanding his habit of reprimanding the objects of his charity, his almsgiving was very indiscriminate. He always gave to beggars, and was never angry when he found he had been imposed upon. While at Trowbridge he was made a magistrate, and was most attentive to the duties of his office.

When Crabbe went to Trowbridge he was in his sixtieth year; but his family seem to have thought that he had some idea of marrying again. In fact he was supposed to have fallen deeply in love with some Wiltshire young lady, and to have written despairing verses on the violence of his passion. It seems that he was very partial to female society, and had a habit of hanging about women, and paying them great attentions, without meaning anything serious. Cowper had the same weakness, which, as we know, was not unnaturally misinterpreted by Lady Unwin. But at least in one instance at Trowbridge, Crabbe was thought to have been in earnest, and his sons looked forward to the prospect of his second marriage with sincere pleasure. Nothing, however, came of it; and very likely the fashionable circles to which he was now about to be introduced drove all other thoughts out of his head.

It was during his second year's residence at Trowbridge that he began his correspondence with Mrs. Leadbeater. Mary Leadbeater was the daughter of Burke's old schoolmaster, Richard Shackleton, who kept a school at Ballitore, in Kildare. William Leadbeater, whom she married in 1791, was another old pupil, and at the time of this correspondence was a prosperous farmer at Ballitore. Crabbe first met her with her father at Burke's house in 1784, when she was still Miss Shackleton, "a pretty, demure lass of twenty-five," standing timidly by while her host read her verses out aloud. She wrote some passable verses, and was also the authoress of "Cottage Dialogues," "Cottage Biography," etc.; and after the publication of the Tales, bethought herself of renewing her acquaintance with one who wrote upon subjects so congenial to her own mind. Mary was a Quaker, and her first letter to Crabbe was dated Ballitore, 7th of 11th month, 1816. Her real object in writing was, as she said, to revive her acquaintance with Crabbe, her excuse being a desire to know whether he drew his characters from nature or imagination. In discussions on this subject, in which she had taken part, she maintained that they were drawn from life. Crabbe now tells her that in a great measure she was correct. His characters, indeed, were not portraits, nor even thinly disguised portraits, like some of Pope's. They were all suggested, in the first instance, by individuals whom he knew. But by changing the situation, the circumstances, and sometimes even the sex, they were too far removed from their originals to be in any danger of recognition. The nearest approach to an exact copy was in "The Borough," the character of Sir Denys Brand being the faithful reproduction of some local "Big-wig," but whether in Leicestershire or Suffolk we are not informed.

The character of Blaney, in the same poem, was taken from a half-pay major on the east coast of Suffolk. It is chiefly for this communication that the correspondence with Mary Leadbeater is valuable in relation to literary history. But there are other passages in the letters which possess great practical interest for us at the present moment, wholly unconnected with literature. One that we refer to is the following, of the date of 1817 :—

" A description of the village society would be gratifying to me— how the manners differ from those in larger societies, or in those under different circumstances. I have observed an extraordinary difference in village manners in England, especially between those places otherwise alike, when there was, and when there was not, a leading man or a squire's family, or a manufactory near, or a populous vitiated town, etc. All these, and many other circumstances, have great influence."

The picture of resident rural proprietors and country clergymen which Crabbe had drawn in his youth, are certainly not such as to warrant the belief that any village would be much better off for their presence. But many things had happened since that time, and he had seen his mistake. Another very interesting passage is that in which the lady points out that Crabbe has shown the real consequences of vice. This is a very just criticism, but relates to a question which must be preserved for future consideration. Crabbe's correspondence with this lady continued down to 1828, and the last letter which he wrote to her was on his seventy-fourth birthday.

His residence in Wiltshire soon made Crabbe acquainted with the Lansdowne family at Bowood, to whom he was introduced by Bowles, the editor of Pope. At Bowood he met Rogers, by whom he was

pressed to come to town the following season, which he
accordingly did, and took lodgings in Bury Street, to be
near to Rogers, who lived in St. James's Place. Crabbe
at once became a member of the brilliant group which
Rogers loved to gather round him, and he must often
have compared, in his own mind, the company which
assembled at Rogers's breakfast-table with that which he
had met at the tables of Burke and Reynolds thirty
years before. It has fallen to the lot of few men to live so
familiarly with two such completely distinct literary circles,
separated from each other by nearly a whole generation,
and still more, perhaps, by the immense political and
social changes which had taken place in the interval.
Crabbe passed at a bound from the atmosphere of "the
Club"—from Johnson, Burke, Reynolds, Langton, and
Boswell, to Byron, Moore, Scott, Campbell, and Canning.
He appeared to the *littérateurs* of the regency as Johnson
appeared to the more prosperous and urbane men
of letters, who succeeded to the Boyces and the
Savages of a past age. He was the last man of
letters of the eighteenth century whom Johnson saw,
and the last of the long line of heroic poets which
Pope and Dryden founded. As such, Crabbe was
regarded by the men of that day with perhaps rather
more than his due share of veneration, though it much
more nearly equalled his deserts than the neglect to
which he was subsequently consigned.

Crabbe now, like Murray, " drank champagne with
the wits." He was one of the three Wiltshire poets—
Bowles and Moore being the other two—whom it was
the fashion to toast ; and whether in town or country, he
was an honoured guest at the houses of all who occupied

the border-land where literature and fashion meet together. He visited at Bowood and Longleat; and if we follow his movements in London by the aid of his own and Moore's Journal, we shall see that he had the *entrée* to some of the best society of the day. At Horace Twiss's he met Lady Cork, Johnson's "lively Miss Monckton," and they must have enjoyed some reminiscences together. He wrote verses to Lady Jersey on her birthday, and seems to have been admitted among the pet lions of Lady Holland. All traces of rusticity had now, we may presume, disappeared from his manners. But he retained to the last one failing, for such it must be called, which was described by a lady to Hallam in the following terms:—"She admitted that Mr. Crabbe was very good cake, only there was such a thick layer of sugar to be cut through before you could get at it." His manner to women seems to have been of the kind called philandering; and there is nothing women hate more.

Crabbe took advantage of the full flush of his position and popularity to publish the "Tales of the Hall," on which he had been diligently at work during the years 1817 and 1818. They appeared in June 1819, and were a great success, Jeffrey preferring them, though this is not the general opinion, to anything which had gone before. Murray at once offered him three thousand pounds for the Tales, together with the copyright of his previous works. Crabbe would have accepted it at once, but some of his friends thought he could do better, and persuaded him to communicate with Longman. Longman, however, offered only one thousand, and Crabbe remained for some time in anything but an enviable frame of mind, fancying that he had allowed the larger sum, which he had already grasped in imagination, to slip through his fingers. Murray, however, adhered to his original offer, for which he was not repaid by the sale of the first edition, and Crabbe was made happy by the receipt of bills for the amount. He was advised to deposit them with a banker, but with a simplicity strange even in Crabbe, he insisted on carrying them down to Trowbridge, in his waist-coat pocket, to show them to his son John, who, otherwise, he said, would not believe in his luck. Contrary to what might have been expected, they reached Trowbridge in safety ; and the eyes of his son John were duly allowed to feast upon them.

At this period of his life Crabbe wrote late at night, and drank weak brandy and water while at work. He also took a great quantity of snuff, portions of which descended on his coat and neck-cloth, and gave him rather a slovenly appearance, though in other respects he was remarkably attentive to his dress. In April 1819 Moore writes in his Journal—"Met Crabbe toddling about the streets of Bath. Whoever would think he was *the* Crabbe?" To what peculiarity in his personal appearance these remarks are pointed I am not assured, unless it was his snuffiness. At this time he was only sixty-four years of age, and we do not hear that he stooped or tottered in his gait. According to Miss Crowfoot, his personal appearance was extremely striking. "No one who met him in the street would have failed to inquire who he was." The next three years were comparatively uneventful ones in Crabbe's life. When he came to London, he made the house of Mr. Hoare, at Hampstead, his head-quarters. Here he became acquainted with Joanna Baillie, who was now in frequent correspondence with Sir Walter Scott, and in the following year, when Scott came to town to see the coronation of George IV., the two poets were at length made known to each other by Mr. Murray.

There is no record remaining of what passed between them on this occasion, except that Scott pressed Crabbe to come to Edinburgh, an invitation which led to his making his appearance there just when Scott was in the thick of the bustle attending the reception of the king. The story is well-known from Lockhart's " Life of Scott." Crabbe, of course, was Scott's guest in Castle Street, and one morning, when Scott came down to breakfast, he found Crabbe and three or four Highland gentlemen trying to talk to each other in French, they mistaking him for a French abbé, and he having taken them for foreigners of some kind, though what he knew not. Crabbe did not stay long at Edinburgh, and was unable to proceed to Abbotsford. It was impossible for him at such a time to see much of Sir Walter Scott himself. But they walked together to Muschat's Cairn, and always had an hour together before going to bed at night.

It fell to Lockhart's lot to lionise Crabbe, and he communicated his reminiscences of the period in a long letter to the poet's son when the latter was preparing his father's biography. From this it appears that Crabbe, in the year 1822, knew no more of Scotland than that it formed the northern part of Britain ; and no more expected to find there men of a different race from the English, speaking a different language, and wearing a different dress, than he would have expected to find them in Cheapside. His astonishment may be imagined. He spent some evenings with Professor Wilson, Hogg, Mackenzie, and Jeffrey, which he seemed to enjoy very much. But it is characteristic of the man that the romance of Edinburgh—" mine own romantic town "—seems to have had few charms for him. He did not care for either the Castle or Holyrood, the rock up which Dundee climbed, the closet in which Rizzio was murdered, the saloon in which Charles Edward danced. When he was taken to Salisbury Crags, he was more engrossed with the stratification of the rock than with the beauty of that splendid prospect. He once told a friend at Trowbridge that he preferred walking in the streets, and watching the faces of the passers-by, to the finest natural scenery ; but, on the other hand, he delighted in the old town, and in wandering about by himself among the wynds and closes, and examining, according to his wont, the dwellings of the poor. Of the Waverley Novels his favourite was *The Heart of Midlothian*, and Effie Deans, who might have figured in the Tales, was a heroine much more after his own heart than either Lucy Ashton or Amy Robsart.

Lockhart tells a story of Wordsworth and Sir George Beaumont, illustrative of Crabbe's supposed want of imagination :— " Crabbe, Sir George Beaumont, and Wordsworth were sitting together in Murray's room in Albemarle Street. Sir George, after sealing a letter, blew out the candle which had enabled him to do so, and, exchanging a look with Wordsworth, began to admire in silence the undulating thread of smoke which slowly arose from the expiring wick, when Crabbe put on the extinguisher." Anne Scott asked if the taper was wax, and, being told it was tallow, seemed to think that Crabbe was in the right. While on the subject of Crabbe's intimacy with Scott, we may as well mention Scott's solitary attempt to imitate Crabbe's style. Canning used always to tell Scott that " Marmion " and " The Lay of the Last Minstrel " could have been better written in the metre of Dryden, and Scott at last resolved to try his hand at it. The result was " The Poacher " (1811), a poem which, as soon as Crabbe saw, he cried out, " This man can do all I can—and something more." Here, however, he was wrong. On the comparative merits of Scott and Crabbe as poets, each in his own line, I am not about to enter; but Crabbe's line was not Scott's, and we have only to compare " The Poacher " with Crabbe's " Smugglers and Poachers," in " Tales of the Hall," to see the difference. Scott's versification is, perhaps, the better of the two; but in force and depth of feeling Crabbe leaves him far behind. Scott, no doubt, was hampered by a metre to which he was unaccustomed. Had he made Black Ned the hero of a ballad, the effect would have been widely different.

Crabbe had still continued to keep up his connection with the family at Belvoir; and after he returned from Scotland, in the autumn of 1822, he received an invitation from the duke, which, unfortunately, he was unable to accept. It appears, however, from the wording of the letter, that he had received several invitations previously, which he had also been obliged to decline. And in the duchess's album, at Belvoir, may be seen several copies of verses by Crabbe, which have never been published, all of a later date than 1820. These are lines on a picture of Powis Castle, by Lady Lucy Clive, and on one of Ludlow Castle, by Lady Harriet Clive, 1822; lines on Stoke Park, 1823; lines on a picture of " Green

Mantle," in " Redgauntlet," by Miss Isabella Forester, 1825; on Guy's Cliff, 1829; and verses on Time and the Duchess of Rutland, without any date. This shows that if he did not visit at the Castle after he went to Trowbridge, he must have been in constant correspondence with its inmates. There is, however, no trace of his having been there during the last eighteen years of his life, either in his own biography, or preserved in the traditions of the family. We can only presume, therefore, that the various subjects were suggested to him in the duchess's letters. The verses I have mentioned have no special merit; the best of those written in the album having been picked out by Mr. George Crabbe for publication.

Crabbe, as I have already stated, continued his annual visits to London down to the year 1825, staying usually with the Hoares at Hampstead, which he sometimes exchanged for the Hummums in Covent Garden, and mixing, as before, in the best literary society of the Metropolis. Among others whom he used frequently to meet were Wilberforce, Joanna Baillie, Miss Edgeworth, Mrs. Siddons, Wordsworth, Southey, Rogers, Lord Holland, etc.; and every season he accompanied the Hoares to some sea-side place—the Isle of Wight, Hastings, and Ilfracombe being their favourite resorts. In the autumn of 1823, he was at Aldeburgh, when he wrote the following verse in his note book :—

> " Then once again, my native place, I come
> Thee to salute, my earliest, latest home ;
> Much are we altered both, but I behold
> In thee a youth renewed, whilst I am old—
> The works of man from dying we may save,
> But man himself moves onward to the grave."

About this time he first saw *Rejected Addresses*, the author of which he had met in society some years before. He thought the parodies ill-natured, but the imitation of his own style excellent. In June 1825 we find him thoroughly enjoying his "season." He has seen all the picture galleries, met all his interesting acquaintances, and has been to Richmond in a steamboat. He reproaches himself with having passed a Sunday in London without going to church ; but he sees no harm in Sunday dinner parties. He says the Garden at Hampstead is "fragrant beyond anything he ever perceived before," and supposes it is what in Persia they called a "Paradisiacal sweetness." It was during this visit that he heard of his being attacked by Hazlitt, in *The Spirit of the Age.* But it does not appear that he ever read the criticism.

Crabbe had now nearly completed his seventy-first year, but so far, with the exception of some severe attacks of neuralgia, from which he occasionally suffered, he had been able thoroughly to enjoy life, and had scarcely felt the approaches of age. It now only remains to tell of his declining years, and the easy and peaceful close of a life which had begun so gloomily, so painfully, and so hopelessly. Some one has said that there are few things more miserable than to look back upon a youth which has not been enjoyed. But Crabbe does not seem to have found it so. His youth and early manhood had passed in wretchedness. But he looked back upon them, at last, without a sigh, and his old age was cheerful and serene.

CHAPTER VI.

CRABBE'S two sons were now married—John to Miss Crowfoot, the daughter of a physician at Beccles, and George to Miss Timbrel, a Trowbridge young lady. Both were clergymen, the elder having the curacy of Pucklechurch, about twenty miles from Trowbridge, and the younger acting as his father's curate. The family circle, therefore, remained comparatively unbroken; and the old man found a constant source of interest and amusement in the society of his grandchildren. His chief friends in the town were Mr. Waldron and Mr. Norris Clarke; and the cities of Bath and Bristol were within easy reach.

The income which he derived from the two livings amounted to about £800 a-year, besides the interest of the £3000 which he had received from Murray; and his family being now established in the world, he was, comparatively speaking, a rich man. He was charitable, hospitable, and liberal, and he eventually succeeded in making a much better impression on his Trowbridge parishioners than he had left behind him at Muston. A little natural irritability he retained to the last. One thing which he particularly disliked was being kept waiting for funerals. One day after having waited for an hour he left the churchyard in a pet, and went home to dinner. Just as he was sitting down a message came that the funeral was waiting for him. The poet showed evident signs of not being in a proper frame of mind for the discharge of such a duty. Whereupon his son John offered to take it for him. " Do so, John," said his father, " you are a milder man than I am."

His chief enjoyment now was to stay with his eldest son at Pucklechurch, spending his mornings, even in the worst weather, in the neighbouring quarries, and returning laden with fossils, which he always laid out in the best bed-room. At other times he would stay with the Hoares in a house which they had taken at Clifton, commanding a fine view over the river Avon ; and he happened to be here in 1831, at the time of the Bristol riots. He wished to go into the town and witness the state of things for himself. But Mr. Hoare would not let him, telling him that clergymen were marked men. Crabbe himself was in favour of the Reform Bill, and predicted that all would be well in the long run if ministers were firm on essentials, and made a few concessions on minor points. I am afraid he and Scott would have been sadly at issue on this question.

In the autumn of 1830, Crabbe was at Hastings, and spent a great deal of his time upon the sands, contemplating all the objects which had been familiar to his youth, and probably conversing with the boatmen, as he had been used to do on the beach at Aldeburgh. The visit lasted from the end of September to some time in November, and it was, we are told, on a dull November morning, with a fresh breeze towards the land, and the big waves bursting in wild foam upon the shingle, that Crabbe looked his last upon the sea. This was as it should be. Crabbe's poetry is redolent of the ocean, but of the ocean under its gloomier and more lowering aspects : not in its tempestuous grandeur, not in its blue and sunny beauty, but swelling moodily under leaden skies, and rolling its turbid waters to the shore in accents of profound melancholy. Such are the scenes from which Crabbe, as we can easily believe, turned slowly and sadly away on that November morning, and returned to Wiltshire for the end.

In the following January (1831) a journey to Beccles was talked about, and in a letter to Mr. Crowfoot, Crabbe gives a very interesting account of his feelings when he last travelled into Suffolk. After saying that he is afraid of the stage coach journey on account of his neuralgia, he proceeds, "And yet I should rejoice to visit Beccles, where everyone is kind to me, and where every object I view has the appearance of friendship and welcome. Beccles is the home of past years, and I could not walk through the streets as a stranger. It is not so at Aldeburgh. There a sadness mixes with all I see or hear ; not a man is living whom I knew in my early portion of life ; my contemporaries are gone, and their successors are unknown to me and I to them. Yet, in my last visit, my niece and I passed an old man, and she said, ' There is one you should know ; you played together as boys, and he looks as if he wanted to tell you so.' Of course I stopped on my way, and Zekiel Thorpe and I became once more acquainted."

The proposed journey never took place, nor yet

another to London, which Crabbe half contemplated in May. In the following autumn, as we have seen, he was at Clifton, and from thence in November went to his son's house at Pucklechurch, where he stayed about a fortnight, and then returned to Trowbridge. While at Pucklechurch he seemed well and strong, and preached twice on Sunday with so much apparent vigour that all who heard him thought he had another ten years to live. His son told him as much. Crabbe's answer was "ten weeks." About two months after his return to Trowbridge he caught a bad cold, which seems to have settled on his chest, and he sunk under it so rapidly that in a few days his recovery was despaired of. A very touching account of his last hours has been left by his biographer, which I need not transcribe here. He died about seven o'clock in the morning on the 3rd of February 1832, having lived rather more than seventy-seven years.

At Trowbridge, on this occasion, his loss was sincerely lamented, for he had become popular at last. Ninety-two of his parishioners, including all the Dissenting ministers of the place, followed him to the grave. The shops were closed, and all the principal inhabitants of the town, dressed in mourning, attended in the church. A subscription was raised to erect a monument to his memory, which was placed in the church in August 1833, with a well-written inscription, which does not exaggerate either his genius or his virtues.

Of Crabbe's character, habits, and social qualifications, we gain from the pages of his biographer a very favourable impression. But that biographer, we must remember, was an affectionate son, who was careful to select from the opinions of his contemporaries whatever did credit to his father. At the same time, it is easy to believe that such failings as he really possessed, and which his son makes no effort to conceal, were due rather to circumstances than to nature—circumstances which attended him till he was nearly thirty years of age, by which time men's characters are formed, and their habits not easily amended.

His conversation, it is said, was not equal to his writings, partly because he was incapable of sustained reasoning, partly because the range of subjects in which he took a real interest was extremely narrow, and partly because he seems early in life to have acquired the habit of not talking about these. If he became involved in an argument he was apt to be soon confused, to wander from the point, and to lose his temper. From having first mixed in society where men like Burke and Johnson led the conversation, he seems to have formed an idea that all conversation should be, more or less, of this character—one superior person taking the lead, and the rest listening and acquiescing. He was ready to listen in his turn to anyone whom he thought had special knowledge, and expected on certain subjects to be listened to himself with equal deference. When this was refused he was dissatisfied and silent.

In the second place, it was difficult to engage him in any general conversation, because there was so little that he cared to talk about. He was not interested in politics —certainly not in the politics of the passing time. He was indifferent to scholarship and philosophy. Of painting, music, and architecture he was equally careless. The talk of the world, as one may call it, concerning the sayings and doings of society, sometimes witty and brilliant, sometimes mere gossip, had no charm for him.   To military and naval subjects, though he lived through the great war, we find scarcely a single allusion in either his biography or his poems. He was no sportsman. No wonder that in the society which he frequented during the last twenty years of his life, he was felt to be ineffective.

It is also on record that he shunned literary conversation, a habit which may be attributed to two separate causes.   In his early youth he had heard literature despised, and had probably come to the conclusion that the less he talked of it the better.   In later years, at the table of the Duke of Rutland, he may have found that such subjects were not always relished by the company ; and in spite of the success which his poetry had then achieved, might sometimes murmur to himself with Goldsmith—

" My shame in crowds my solitary pride."

It appears, however, from the testimony of Mr. Duncan, a gentleman who frequently met him at the Hoares, at Hampstead, that in his later years his colloquial powers had improved.   He says that he avoided saying witty things when he could have done so, for fear of wounding the feelings of anyone present ; but that his conversation was easy, fluent, and well-informed ; while other witnesses assure us that it was rich in shrewd and sagacious observations on human nature.   One of his admirers, indeed, at Trowbridge, Mr. Norris Clarke, went so far as to say that it was as well worth preserving as Dr. Johnson's. Moore, however, is the best judge, and it is from him we learn the impression which Crabbe created in the best literary society.

His manners in society, after he had once become used to it, are said to have been singularly pleasing, and to have fully justified the saying of his early patron, that he had the "mind and feelings of a gentleman." Great simplicity and kindliness, mingled with an element of ceremonious politeness, which he must have acquired in Charles Street and at Beaconsfield, were the leading characteristics of his address, and they caused him, as may easily be imagined, to be a great favourite with children. This report of his demeanour is fully borne out by his portrait, taken in 1817 by Thomas Phillips, R.A. He is dressed in the high collared coat of the period, with the loose unstiffened cravat which belonged to an earlier era, his white hair carefully rolled back, and the smile on his countenance, though rather too much like a set smile, we can easily believe to have been attractive. The general expression of the countenance is placid, though by no means destitute of shrewdness, and the desire to please, which is very apparent in the eyes, is balanced by a sarcastic mouth, which tells its own story. There is another portrait of him by Pickersgill, which I have not seen.

Of Crabbe's method of work, we are only told that he thought autumn the most favourable season of the year for poetical composition—an idea which corresponds with the autumnal character of his poetry ; and that he was always greatly stimulated by a snowstorm. "Sir Eustace Grey" was written during a great fall of snow, which kept him confined in the house. In every walk that he took, however, and in all his botanical and geological expeditions, he always carried some verses in his head, which he corrected and developed, with the aid of his note-book, as he went along. There is no doubt that his heart was thoroughly in his work ; and that in his own estimation of himself, though far from an overweening one, he was nothing if not a poet.

When he was at Glemham he was thought a popular preacher, and his manner in the pulpit was familiar and colloquial.

Several of Crabbe's descendants are still living. His eldest son, George, who married Miss Timbrel, and eventually settled on the living of Bredfield, in Norfolk, died in 1857, leaving a son George, who married his cousin, a daughter of John Crabbe, and was presented to the living of Merton, also in the county of Norfolk. His daughter married, May 20th, 1885, Mr. Rivet Carnac, the Rector of Tong, in Shropshire. This lady has two maiden aunts, I believe, still living at Brighton, and an uncle in Australia.

CHAPTER VII.

THE question has been sometimes asked whether Crabbe was either a great poet or a great writer. If he was the first he was the second. But as a judicial answer to the whole question would involve an. elaborate inquiry into the nature and characteristics of true poetry, far beyond the limits proper to the present volume, I prefer to rest his claims to greatness on the testimony of competent authorities, to which my own opinion, after all, can add little or no weight. A long array of illustrious names, extending over more than a century, critics and poets of the most opposite schools, yet all unanimous on this one point, may, I think, be accepted as sufficient evidence in his favour, without any further argument on the subject. Burke and Fox, Johnson and Reynolds, Gifford, Jeffrey, and Wilson, Jane Austen and Sir Walter Scott, Byron, Wordsworth, and Rogers, Lord Tennyson and Cardinal Newman, all alike bear witness to his genius. All recognise in Crabbe the vigorous creative faculty, the power of rhythmical expression, the command over the passions, and the knowledge of the human heart, which are the essential

constituents of a real and great poet. Many modern
readers might reject the authority of critics whom it is
the fashion to pronounce obsolete if their voices stood
alone; but when confirmed by the testimony of others,
whom modern literature delights to honour, they are
entitled not only to all the respect which they commanded
in their own day, but to the additional weight which they
derive from agreement with a later age, governed by new
canons of taste, and owning allegiance to a different style.

What Johnson said of "The Village," I have already
recorded. In the opinion of Jeffrey, Crabbe was the
author of "some of the most original and powerful
poetry which the world ever saw." Gifford thinks his
landscape superior to Goldsmith's in "distinctness, ani-
mation, and firmness of touch," and gives high praise to
the "sublimity" and "grandeur" of his "Storm at Sea."
Professor Wilson says, "Crabbe is confessedly the most
original and vivid painter of the vast varieties of common
life that England has ever produced;" and, again, "In all
the poetry of this extraordinary man, we see a constant
display of the passions as they are excited and exacer-
bated by the customs, laws, and institutions of society."
From Rogers's "Italy" these lines have often been
quoted:—

> " Had I thy pencil, Crabbe (when thou hast done,
>   Late may it be . . . it will, like Prospero's staff,
>   Be buried fifty fathoms in the earth),
>   I would portray the Italian—now I cannot."

Wordsworth, who first became acquainted with
Crabbe's poetry in the same way as Sir Walter Scott, by
reading the extract from "The Village" which Burke

quoted in the *Annual Register*, said that Crabbe's poetry would last "from its combined merits as truth and poetry fully as long as anything that has been expressed in verse since it first made its appearance." Byron, besides what he said in "English Bards and Scotch Reviewers,"—*i.e.*, that Crabbe was "Nature's sternest painter, and her best,"—declared, in 1816, that he considered Crabbe and Coleridge "the first of these times in point of power and genius." In 1820 he called him "the first of living poets." Lord Tennyson* is reported to have said of Crabbe that he "lived in a world of his own," and he has singled out for special admiration a passage in "Tales of the Hall"—marvellously illustrative of "the pathetic fallacy," in which the dejected lover looks out upon a dull October morning, and sees in the landscape the reflection of his own sadness.

> " Early he rose, and looked with many a sigh
> On the red light that fill'd the eastern sky ;
> Oft had he stood before, alert and gay,
> To hail the glories of the new-born day ;
> But now dejected, listless, languid, low,
> He saw the wind upon the water blow,
> And the cold stream curl'd onward as the gale
> From the pine hill blew harshly down the vale.
> On the right side the youth a wood survey'd,
> With all its dark intensity of shade ;
> Where the rough wind alone was heard to move,
> In this, the pause of nature and of love,
> When now the young are rear'd and when the old,
> Lost to the tie, grow negligent and cold :

* *Readings from Crabbe*, by Mr. E. Fitzgerald. Mr. Fitzgerald, who only died three years ago, was a great friend of Lord Tennyson, who dedicated "Tiresias" to him, and he was also very intimate with both the son and grandson of Crabbe.

> Far to the left he saw the tents of men,
> Half hid in mist that hung upon the fen ;
> Before him swallows, gathering for the sea,
> Took their short flights, and twitter'd on the lea ;
> And near the bean sheaf stood, the harvest done,
> And slowly blackened in the sickly sun ;
> All these were sad in nature, or they took
> Sadness from him, the likeness of his look."

The touch of colour in the bean sheaf is exquisite. I have already quoted Cardinal Newman, to whom Crabbe was delightful in his youth, and is still more delightful in his age. Jane Austen thought she could have married him. The Waverley Novels are full of quotations from Crabbe ; and his poetry soothed the last hours of both Walter Scott and Charles Fox.

It is impossible to explain away this great accumulation of evidence. When all deductions have been made, which may be due to the operation of literary motives and controversies—and they are not inconsiderable— enough will remain to secure him a place among the immortals while English poetry continues to be read, if not when it has ceased to be written.

That of the eulogies bestowed on Crabbe by Jeffrey and Byron, some part was due to the peculiar position which he occupied in English literature, and the help which he afforded to the orthodox school of critics in their war with the reformers, I think it is impossible to doubt. He came at a time when Pope's authority was trembling in the balance ; when a new literary taste was gradually springing up, doubtful whether it could be satisfied with the canons of the Augustan age ; and when the demand for a return to nature, created by a literary reaction, was seconded for a time by the delusive plausibilities of a political revolution. It was at this moment that Crabbe appeared upon the stage, with the welcome assurance in his mouth that the world might gratify its new cravings without abandoning its old idols, and enjoy truth and nature without loss of classical dignity. To men like Byron and Jeffrey his appearance was a god-send; the one on behalf of Pope, the other in rebuke of Wordsworth, could both appeal equally to Crabbe. Did the public ask for truth, nature, simplicity, for the genius which sees poetry in the "incidents and situations of common life,"* here they were, in the orthodox garb, and expressed in that poetic diction which Johnson himself had prescribed. Did they ask whether the heroic metre was equal to the wider sympathies and more scrupulous literary accuracy of the new generation, here was their answer.

Byron declares that English poetry has been steadily on the decline since the depreciation of Pope set in, and points to Crabbe as the sole remaining hope of a degenerate age. Jeffrey contrasts Martha Ray, in "The Thorn," with Phœbe Dawson in the "Register," and triumphantly asks whether the shadowy being of Wordsworth can be compared for a moment with the graphic and highly-finished scenes, and the living, breathing human beings which Crabbe sets before us in "the manner of the great masters." "Wordsworth," he says, most unjustly, "has contrived to tell us nothing of the unfortunate fair one, but that her name is Martha Ray, and that she goes up to the top of a hill, in a red cloak, and cries 'Oh, misery.'" Wordsworth has contrived to

* Preface to Wordsworth's *Lyrical Ballads.*

tell us a great deal more than this. Martha Ray is a
triumph of suggestion, like the knocking in "Macbeth,"
or the sound of Ravenswood's boot grinding on the floor
of the room during his last night of agony at Wolf's
Crag. But the contrast served the critic's turn, and
illustrates his theory well enough. Fortunately Crabbe
stands in no need of any foil, and we are not
obliged to accept Jeffrey's estimate of Wordsworth to
justify our love of Crabbe ; nor need our admiration of
"The Village" and "The Borough" be diminished by
discovering that Jeffrey's praise was not disinterested.
If, in his anxiety to depreciate one poet, he has ex-
tolled another more highly than he otherwise would have
done, the fact may shake our confidence in Jeffrey, not
our estimate of Crabbe. All that Jeffrey says might
be quite true, though he might not have said so much
had Wordsworth not been there to prick him on.

Crabbe certainly did succeed in combining the
characteristics of the Twickenham school and the
Lake school, and in showing that the art of the one
and the naturalness of the other were capable of
being united. With a power of versification scarcely
inferior to Dryden's, he united a depth of feeling
which neither Pope nor Dryden ever knew. If
Crabbe's characters had been portraits of distinguished
living statesmen, women of fashion, and men of letters,
they would have been as well known as Sporus,
Atticus, and Atossa : while in Crabbe's descriptions
of nature there is a minute pre-Raphaelite accuracy,
which, in his hands, so far from injuring the general
effect, enhances it, and is to be found in no other
English poet who has written in the same metre.

Even Thomson's "Seasons" are not so "real" as Crabbe.

It may be thought, perhaps, that in what has been said of Crabbe injustice has been done to Cowper. It is curious that the two men seem to have known so little of each other. They started on their literary career together. "The Library" was published in June 1781, and Cowper's first volume in March 1782. The two appeared simultaneously as candidates for public favour. When Crabbe was dining every day with Burke and Reynolds, it is impossible that he should not have heard Cowper talked about. *The Critical* and the *Monthly Reviews*, which Crabbe would be pretty sure to read, contained notices of him. Thurlow, who became Crabbe's friend, and was intimate with the circle in which he moved, was also Cowper's friend. There was so much to bring the two men together, yet there is so little to show that they had the slightest knowledge of each other.

The truth is, that Cowper did not occupy at all the the same position as Crabbe. Not only did he move in a more contracted sphere, but he did not present himself to the world as a disciple of the Augustan school. In enumerating the poets who had handed down the torch to the beginning of the present century, Byron does not include Cowper. Cowper wrote admirably in rhyme, though his best-known works are in blank verse. But it is not the rhyme of Pope or Campbell. It is as different from these as the hexameters of Catullus are from the hexameters of Virgil. Cowper, in fact, claimed rather to be the founder of a new school; whereas it was Crabbe's glory *stare super vias antiquas*. Cowper had much of the simplicity and reality which the Lake school required, as well as Crabbe ; but then in Cowper it was purchased by the sacrifice of the old style. In Crabbe, it was not. He combined rare fidelity to nature with a highly artificial mode of expression.

Further than that, while Cowper surpassed Crabbe in refinement, gentleness, and spiritual fervour, he was infinitely inferior to Crabbe in his knowledge of human nature, and power of delineating individuals. He never attempted tales, and I cannot think any of his characters in the "Progress of Error," "Truth," "Hope," and "Conversation," equal to those in "The Borough" and "Tales of the Hall." Moreover, he did not look round him with the observant glance of Crabbe, who, as Lockhart says, never opened his eyes in vain. Like many other invalids, or hypochondriacs, surrounded with comforts themselves, he had little deep sympathy with physical suffering and hardship. He too, like Crabbe, understood the falsity of those conventional pictures of rural felicity to which the world had so long been accustomed. And there are lines in the "Winter Evening" following out much the same train of thought as we find in the opening of "The Village." Sometimes, indeed, the resemblance is so close as to suggest something more than a merely accidental coincidence. "The Village" was published in May 1783, and "The Task" in June 1785, and the reference to the golden age of Maro, which occurs in both, might warrant the conjecture that the author of the later poem was no stranger to the earlier. So too Cowper's lines—

> " The frugal housewife trembles when she lights
> Her scanty stock of brushwood,"

are very near to Crabbe's—

> " Or her, that matron pale, whose trembling hand
> Throws on the wretched hearth the expiring brand."

But be that as it may, Cowper's grasp of the subject is very different from Crabbe's. He too describes the interior of a labourer's cottage, "and the misery of a stinted meal." But in what a different tone ! In Cowper we see only the gentle compassion of a kind-hearted gentleman for trials which he regarded as inevitable. In Crabbe we see the *sæva indignatio* of the satirist, angry with a world and a society in which such things could be, and with the lying poets who had so long disguised the truth. 'Moreover, Cowper's picture of the agricultural labourer is, on the whole, a cheerful one. The waggoner and his horses, the woodman and his dog, the wife and her poultry, are all described in tones which rather favour than condemn those views of rural life which Crabbe had set himself to expose. Had Crabbe described the waggoner or the woodman, we should have heard something about ague, rheumatism, and fever.

They cannot, therefore, well be compared together. It is as a great religious poet that we must continue to admire Cowper, the poet who threw himself heart and soul into the great evangelical revival of a hundred years ago, and did for Wesley and Wilberforce what Keble did for Newman and Pusey. In this great work his style and method necessarily partook of the protest which he was uttering against the stagnant orthodoxy of the period ; and it was this, I think, more than any conscious literary convictions, which carried him away from the school of Pope and Johnson. The Lakists never seem

to have heartily recognised him as a labourer in the same
vineyard; and as a painter of middle-class characters
and peasant life, he can hardly be said to come into
competition with Crabbe.

It has been necessary to say these few words on the
position of Cowper, because, at first sight, it might
appear that he and Crabbe travelled along the same
road, and represented the same class of ideas. Nothing
can be more untrue. They touch each other at certain
points. But they neither start from the same source, nor
make for the same port, nor, as I have already said,
belong to the same school. My own opinion is that the
English writer with whom Crabbe has most in common
is George Eliot. The story of Hetty Sorel he would
have told to perfection. Mr. Dempster, Squire Cass,
Mr. Tulliver, are all characters after Crabbe's own
heart; and the mingled village tragedy and comedy,
with the vices, virtues, and humours of the middle class,
which George Eliot understood so well, were equally
familiar to the author of the " Parish Register " and the
" Tales in Verse."

Crabbe, however, did not take his place at first among
the poets of character and manners. His literary
activity, as far, at least, as the world knew anything of
it, may be divided into three periods. " The Library,"
" The Village," and " The Newspaper," the products of
this first period, possess characters of their own quite
distinct from all that followed. " The Library " is
simply a description of literature, under the various
heads of history, divinity, philosophy, law, poetry, and
romance. The lines in which the poet, at this time in
his twenty-eighth year, describes the loss of faith in the

vision which had beguiled his boyhood, ghosts, fairies, demons, mysterious castles, and enchanted forests, are a very favourable specimen of his earlier style, and possess great merit.

> " But lost, for ever lost, to me these joys,
>   Which reason scatters, and which time destroys ;
>   Too dearly bought : maturer judgment calls
>   My busied mind from tales and madrigals ;
>   My doughty giants all are slain or fled,
>   And all my knights, blue, green, or yellow, dead !
>   No more the midnight fairy tribe I view,
>   All in the merry moonshine tippling dew ;
>   E'en the last lingering fiction of the brain,
>   The churchyard ghost is now at rest again ;
>   And all the wayward wanderings of my youth
>   Fly reason's power, and shun the light of truth."

" The Newspaper," published in March 1785, is the least interesting of the three poems, though a clever satire on the class of newspapers to which Mr. Puff was a contributor. It winds up with an exhortation to all aspiring youths who have dabbled in poetry to return to some more profitable trade, and as the poet took his own advice, and published nothing more for twenty-two years, we may presume that he was in earnest.

" The Village," which is *facile princeps* among his earlier performances, has indeed a charm of its own in which the riper productions of his later years, however superior in other respects, are necessarily deficient. For in " The Village " we have the man himself. " The Library " and " The Newspaper " are, after all, little more than academic prolusions such as many living poets could have written, and written just as well

as Crabbe. But " The Village " is racy of the soil. It
is all his own. In it he pours forth the accumulated
melancholy and bitterness of ten years of misery. Here
he first exhibits those powers in virtue of which he takes
his true rank in literature—the powers of a great satirist—
put forth against a social falsehood, which fills him with
righteous wrath. As with most satirists, he exaggerates
the error which he considers it his mission to combat,
but still it was a real one, and as connected with one of
the most important social questions of the present day, it
has a deep interest for ourselves.

The condition of the agricultural labourer at the close
of the American War had deteriorated greatly from what
it was at the end of the reign of George the Second.
The best account of the various fluctuations in his
fortunes, and his downward progress during the latter part
of the eighteenth century, with which I am acquainted,
is to be found in the Report of the " Commissioners
appointed to inquire into the employment of women and
children in agriculture " (1867), of which I have made
great use in an account of the agricultural labourer
published by myself a year ago; and from this we may
easily see, by comparing the rate of wages and the cost
of commodities at the two periods, that between the position of the labourer in 1750 and 1790 there was the
whole difference between comfort and indigence. I am
not sure that before the earlier of these two dates there
might not have been some truth in the conventional
conception of it, which Crabbe attacked so fiercely.
Wages were high in proportion to the cost of necessaries.
The cottager, with his rights of common, had plenty of
elbow room. He brewed his own beer, kept his cow

and his pig, had plenty of milk and bacon, and, if we can trust Cobbett, was thoroughly contented with his lot.* But with the enclosure of the commons, and the rise in prices which followed the American war, his troubles began, and they soon attracted the attention of practical philanthropists. A society was formed in 1796 by Mr. Wilberforce and Mr. Thomas Bernard for improving the condition of the labourer, and "renewing his connection with the land"—and in this association lay the germ of the allotment system. When Crabbe was growing up to manhood the labourers were just experiencing the commencement of this disastrous change in their condition; but the old language continued to be used, and as Crabbe probably thought, had the effect of diverting public opinion from the real truth, and preventing remedial measures from being taken.

Dr. Johnson, we are told, was delighted with "The Village," because it harmonised with all his own sentiments as to the "false notions of rustic happiness and rustic virtue." These false notions, however, seem to have been rather a tradition derived from a time when there was some truth in them than the result of direct misrepresentation by the poets, though they were commonly imputed to the latter. In Crabbe's time, however, they were very wide of the truth. We must remember, too, that it was not only the figment of rustic happiness at which

---

* "The opening of the birch leaves is the signal for the pheasant to begin to crow, the blackbird to whistle, and the thrush to sing. . . . These are among the means which Providence has benignantly appointed to sweeten the toils by which food and raiment are produced; these the English ploughman could once hear without the sorrowful feeling that he himself was a pauper."

Crabbe levelled his shafts, but the figment also of rustic innocence. He wished to draw a correct picture of the labouring poor in contrast with the imaginary one, which had long done duty for the real. If he was angry with those who seemed to keep up the delusion, that what was really a miserable lot in life was a happy one, he had no less contempt for those who allowed themselves to believe, that because the peasant was wretched he must necessarily be virtuous, and that because he was unused to towns he must therefore be ignorant of crime. He would tell the whole truth. He would paint the poor as they really were. If he asked us to compassionate their poverty, he was not justified in throwing a veil over their vices. Crabbe, in fact, was too much in earnest to be otherwise than perfectly truthful. He scorned to trick out the real sufferings and sorrows of the peasantry in borrowed plumes, or to make them the subject of poetic embellishment and embroidery—

"The tinsel trappings of poetic pride."

I have said that he exaggerated the evil : and we may see that his subsequent experience at Muston and Glem-ham modified the impressions which he had originally derived from Aldeburgh and the villages in the immediate neighbourhood. The picture which he gives us in "The Village," however faithful to what Crabbe actually saw, was never a fair picture of the English peasantry in general, even at their lowest ebb. It was none the less useful, perhaps, as a protest against a general error. But it was only strictly accurate of a particular locality. Crabbe was to some extent aware of this, as will be seen in the following extract, but he did not realise it fully till a later period of his life. As his description of the agricultural labourer, and the original and independent line which he struck out for himself in dealing with the subject, are marked points in his career, I must here present the reader with a rather long quotation—

" Nor you, ye poor, of letter'd scorn complain,
To you the smoothest song is smooth in vain ;
O'ercome by labour, and bow'd down by time,
Feel you the barren flattery of a rhyme?
Can poets soothe you, when you pine for bread
By winding myrtles round your ruin'd shed?
Can their light tales your weighty griefs o'erpower,
Or glad with airy mirth the toilsome hour?
   Lo, where the heath, with withering brake grown o'er,
Lends the light turf that warms the neighbouring poor ;
From thence a length of burning sand appears,
Where the thin harvest waves its wither'd ears ;
Rank weeds that every art and care defy,
Reign o'er the land, and rob the blighted rye ;
There thistles stretch their prickly arms afar,
And to the ragged infant threaten war ;
There poppies nodding, mock the hope of toil ;
There the blue bugloss paints the sterile soil ;
Hardy and high, above the slender sheaf,
The slimy mallow waves her silky leaf ;
O'er the young shoot the charlock throws a shade,
And clasping tares cling round the sickly blade ;
With mingled tints the rocky coasts abound,
And a sad splendour vainly shines around.
   But these are scenes where Nature's rugged hand
Gave a spare portion to the famish'd land ;
Hers is the fault, if here mankind complain
Of fruitless toil and labour spent in vain ;
But yet in other scenes more fair in view,
Where Plenty smiles—alas ! she smiles for few—
And those who taste not, yet behold her store,

Are as the slaves that dig the golden ore,
The wealth around them makes them doubly poor.

Or will you deem them amply paid in health,
Labour's fair child, that languishes with wealth?
Go then! and see them rising with the sun,
Through a long course of daily toil to run;
See them beneath the dog-star's raging heat,
When the knees tremble and the temples beat;
Behold them leaning on their scythes; look o'er
The labour past, and toils to come explore;
See them alternate suns and showers engage,
And hoard up aches and anguish for their age;
Thro' fens and marshy moors their steps pursue,
When their warm pores imbibe the evening dew;
Then own that labour may as fatal be
To these thy slaves as thine excess to thee.
Amid this tribe too oft a manly pride
Strives in strong toil the fainting heart to hide.
There may you see the youth of slender frame
Contend with weakness, weariness, and shame;
Yet urged along and proudly loth to yield,
He strives to join his fellows of the field:
Till long contending nature droops at last,
Declining health rejects his poor repast,
His cheerless spouse the coming danger sees,
And mutual murmurs urge the slow disease.

Yet grant them health, 'tis not for us to tell,
Though the head droops not, that the heart is well;
Or will you praise that homely, healthy fare,
Plenteous and plain, that happy peasants share;
Oh, trifle not with wants you cannot feel,
Nor mock the misery of a stinted meal;
Homely, not wholesome, plain, not plenteous, such
As you who praise would never deign to touch.

Ye gentle souls who dream of Rural ease,
Whom the smooth streams and smoother sonnets please:
Go! if the peaceful cot your praises snare,
Go look within, and ask if Peace be there;

> If peace be his—that drooping weary Sire;
> Or theirs, that Offspring round their feeble fire;
> Or hers, that Matron pale, whose trembling hand
> Turns on the wretched hearth the expiring brand."

The descriptive lines which form the first half of the above passage are an excellent example of Crabbe's close observation of nature, combined with his still more remarkable faculty of bringing the minutest details under the yoke of rhyme, without blurring or confusing them. Thomson was as close an observer, but then he had all the freedom of blank verse in which to expatiate. Goldsmith has given us some Dutch pictures represented in immortal rhymes, but they cannot compare with Crabbe's for profusion and variety. Tennyson, I think, is the only English poet who has approached Crabbe in this particular combination of beauties; and Tennyson employs measures which are much more easily adapted to pictures of this kind than heroics. For the description of nature in heroic verse, Crabbe, I think, is unrivalled among English poets.

The latter portion of the above passage embodies that conception of the agricultural poor with which Crabbe started in life, and reflects the mood of his own mind when he saw everything around him with a jaundiced eye, and in its worst colours. At this time, moreover, Crabbe had little other experience of rural life than what he derived from the population of his native district, half fishermen and half labourers, sometimes smugglers and sometimes poachers. Into *their* cottages he had penetrated, and witnessed with his own eyes what he describes in "The Village."

It is probable that he saw nothing while at Wickham, or Woodbridge, or during his early visits to Beccles and Parham, to correct these impressions. At these places he did not make himself familiarly acquainted with the peasantry, as he had done at home ; and naturally took it for granted that they were all alike. It was not till his duties as a clergyman led him into the cottages of the better class of agricultural labourers, well cared for by resident proprietors, that he saw there were two sides to the picture. He still held his ground against the idealists, and maintained that the agricultural labourer was neither happier nor better than the mechanic or artisan. But he saw that his condition was not one of unmixed wretchedness, without light or hope, and in the " Parish Register " we find an amended version of " The Village." We have vice and misery, but we have also " fair scenes of peace." The leaden gloom which lowers over " The Village " is lifted in " The Parish," and the sun makes its way through the clouds.

To the subject matter of "The Village" no exception can be taken. The life of the husbandman has in all ages of the world been held a proper subject for poetry. The moral, though overcharged, is on the whole just. The versification and language are singularly pleasing, though not free from blemishes which continued to disfigure his style to the end of his life. His grammar is not always correct, and his meaning is sometimes so obscure as to be nearly unintelligible. In the lines—

> " No cast by nature on a frowning coast
> Which neither groves nor happy valleys boast."

There is a false concord, for boast ought certainly to be boasts ; and in the following—

> " Or will you deem them amply paid in health
> Labour's fair child that languishes with wealth."

It is difficult to understand what is meant by the second line. How any child of labour, properly so called, whether fair or foul, can be said to languish with wealth, I do not quite perceive ; or if Crabbe means that the child of labour, whom health makes fair, would lose his health if he became rich and idle, then either "them" in the first line should be "him," or "child" in the second line should be "children." I mention these mistakes at once to avoid the necessity of calling attention to them further on. I wish they were not so easily to be found.

More than twenty years, as we have seen, passed away between the publication of "The Newspaper" and the publication of the "Parish Register," with which the second period of Crabbe's literary career opens. But it must not be supposed that he had been idle all the time. In the year 1779 he had ready for publication matter enough to fill another volume, consisting of one poem on the story of Naaman, another to be called "Gipsy Will," and a third founded on a local legend, "The Pedlar of Swaffham." But by the advice of his friend, Mr. Turner, he laid them aside, and set to work upon the "Parish Register." This poem, like "The Village," is confined to strictly rural life, and reproduces his experience of Muston and Glemham. But, unlike "The Village," it consists of a series of little stories, or narratives, suggested by the various entries of baptisms, marriages, and

funerals, which " The Register " contains; and here
Crabbe for the first time reveals his great powers as a
painter of manners and character, and that depth of feeling which Jeffery, somewhat unmeaningly, terms "plebeian
pathos." How pathos can be either plebeian or patrician
it is difficult to understand. This, then, is what distinguishes the three earlier poems, published between
1781 and 1785, from the three which followed, published between 1807 and 1812. The former are
poems of description. The latter, while still exclusively
exhibiting the same descriptive skill, are poems of
character, the circumstances being sometimes sufficiently
extended and complicated to deserve the appellation of
a plot.

Part I. of the " Parish Register," "Baptisms," begins
with that more agreeable version of the peasant's life to
which I have already referred, and presents us with a
variety of rustic incident which need not be specified in
detail. The best passage in it is the account of the
poor farmer, and the kind of jests in which his richer
neighbours indulge at his expense. Here Crabbe holds
up to nature a mirror without speck or flaw.

In Part II., " Marriages," occurs the story of
Phœbe Dawson, to which I have already alluded, and
which was so great a favourite with Charles Fox in his
dying hours. It might, perhaps, be objected to Crabbe's
pictures of the poor, that stories of seduction and illicit
love figure in them too frequently. But those who are
acquainted with the state of our country parishes under
the old Poor Law will know that he is guilty of little
misrepresentation, though to harp on this one theme so
constantly as he does, may perhaps be a defect in art.

But superior to Phœbe Dawson, I think, is the description of the wedding which precedes it, and of which the truthfulness is almost dreadful. The boy, much against his will, has been compelled to marry the girl who is really fond of him ; and here they stand before the altar—

> " Next at our altar stood a luckless pair,
> Brought by strong passions and a warrant there ;
> By long rent cloak, hung loosely, strove the bride
> From every eye what all perceived to hide,
> While the boy bridegroom, shuffling in his place,
> Now hid awhile, and now exposed his face ;
> As shame alternately with anger strove,
> The brain confused with muddy ale, to move.
> In haste and stammering he performed his part,
> And look'd the rage that rankled in his heart ;
> (So will each lover inly curse his fate,
> Too soon made happy and made wise too late) ;
> I saw his features take a savage gloom,
> And deeply threaten for the days to come.
> Low spake the lass, and lisp'd and minced the while,
> Look'd on the lad, and faintly tried to smile ;
> With softened speech, and humbled love, she strove,
> To stir the embers of departed love :
> While he, a tyrant, frowning walked before,
> Felt the poor purse, and sought the public door ;
> She, sadly following, in submission went,
> And saw the final shilling foully spent ;
> Then to her father's hut the pair withdrew,
> And bade to love and comfort long adieu ! "

The third part of " The Register," entitled, " Burials," contains one or two very finely-drawn characters. But it is chiefly remarkable for the tenderness with which the poet describes the death and funeral of the mother of a family suddenly snatched away, after a short illness, which had seized her in the full enjoyment of health and strength.

" Called not away when time had loosed each hold
On the fond heart, and each desire grew cold ;
But when, to all that knit us to our kind,
She felt fast bound, as charity can bind :—
Not when the ills of age, its pain, its care,
The drooping spirit for its fate prepare ;
And each affection failing, leaves the heart
Loosed from life's charm, and willing to depart ;
But all her ties the strong invader broke,
In all their strength by one tremendous stroke !
Sudden and swift the eager pest came on,
And terror grew, till every hope was gone ;
Still those around appeared for hope to seek !
But view'd the sick and were afraid to speak.

.   .   .   .

Slowly they bore with solemn steps the dead,
When grief grew loud and bitter tears were shed.
The elder sister strove her pangs to hide,
And soothing words to younger minds applied :
' Be still, be patient ;' oft she strove to say,
But failed as oft, and weeping, turned away.

.   .   .   .

Arrived at home, how then they gazed around
On every place—where she—no more was found ;—
The seat at table she was wont to fill ;
The fire-side chair, still set, but vacant still ;
The garden-walks, a labour all her own ;
The latticed bower, with trailing shrubs o'ergrown ;
The Sunday pew she filled with all her race—
Each place of hers was now a sacred place—
Oh, sacred sorrow ! by which souls are tried,
Sent not to punish mortals but to guide,

> If thou art mine (and who shall proudly dare
> To tell his maker he has had his share ?),
> Still let me feel for what thy pangs are sent,
> And be my guide, and not my punishment."

" The Borough " is a poem in twenty-four letters, in which is set before us almost every variety of life and incident which an English country-town is capable of affording—the clergy, the parish clerk, the Dissenters, the politicians, the lawyers, the doctors, the tradesmen, the amusements of the place, clubs and inns, the theatre and the school, the almshouse, the workhouse, the hospital, the poor and their dwellings, and, finally and appropriately, the prison, *nostriest farrago belli.* Crabbe's works would have produced a better effect had " The Village " and " Parish Register " been thrown into one, so as to form a companion picture to the longer poem. This and " The Borough " together would then have furnished us with a complete and symmetrical representation of provincial life. We have the reality ; but we might as well have had the name.

Of the three poems which mark the middle period of Crabbe's fertility, " The Borough " is undoubtedly the best, and some prefer it to everything else that he has written. While particular passages may be quoted from " Tales of the Hall " superior to anything in " The Borough," the latter exhibits the more complete combination of his various excellences. His power over the passions of terror and pity are nowhere more conspicuous than in his picture of the condemned cell, the storm at sea, and the return of the consumptive sailor to die in the arms of his betrothed. I have always thought Crabbe's condemned felon, though not free from his characteristic blemishes, among the finest and most powerfully-written scenes in English poetry. The clergyman of the parish visits him in his cell, and thus records his observation :—

> " Each sense was palsied ; when he tasted food,
> He sigh'd, and said, ' Enough—'tis very good.'
> Since his dread sentence, nothing seemed to be
> As once it was—he seeing, could not see,
> Nor hearing, hear aright ;—when first I came
> Within his view, I fancied there was shame,
> I judged resentment ; I mistook the air—
> These fainter passions live not with despair ;
> Or but exist and die :—Hope, fear, and love,
> Joy, doubt, and hate, may other spirits move,
> But touch not his, who every waking hour
> Has one fixed dread, and always feels its power."

He then goes on to describe the condemned man's dream. Such dreams have often been described before ; but there is, I think, a peculiar beauty in the following. He dreams that he is walking in the garden of his former home with the village-girl by his side, to whom he has just told his love :—

> " All now is pleasant ;—'tis a moment's gleam
> Of former sunshine—stay, delightful dream !
> Let him within his pleasant garden walk,
> Give him her arm, of blessings let them talk.
>
> .   .   .   .
>
>   Pierced by no crime, and urged by no desire
> For more than true and honest hearts require,
> They feel the calm delight, and thus proceed
> Through the green lane—then linger in the mead—
> Stray o'er the heath in all its purple bloom,
> And pluck the blossom where the wild bees hum ;
> Then through the broomy bound with ease they pass,
> And press the sandy sheep-walk's slender grass,

Where dwarfish flowers among the gorse are spread,
And the lamb browses by the linnet's bed.
Then 'cross the bounding brook they make their way
O'er its rough bridge—and there behold the bay !

. . . Now, arm in arm, now parted, they behold
The glittering waters on the shingles roll'd :
The timid girls half dreading their design,
Dip the small foot in the retarded brine,
And search for crimson weeds, which spreading flow,
Or lie like pictures on the sands below :

Tokens of bliss !—' Oh, horrible ! a wave
Roars as it rises—save me, Edward ! save !'
She cries—Alas ! the watchman on his way
Calls, and lets in—truth, terror, and the day."

There is only one objection to be taken to this passage, and it is this—that we do not in dreams either see so many objects, or see them so minutely, as the unfortunate criminal is here supposed to do. Crabbe's love of making an inventory is very conspicuous in this fine passage, and would have been more so had I given the whole of it.

Crabbe's severe analysis of human motives, his perception of the meaner springs of action, which often take the appearance of magnanimity and munificence, are seen in their greatest perfection in the character of Sir Denys Brand, while in Swallow, the attorney, who, having grown rich,

" Took a village seat,
And like a vulture looked abroad for meat,"

we have a less elaborate but still admirable satirical portrait. The poet's sense of humour, his command of comedy as well as tragedy, less often visible in his poetry, readily provoke our laughter in the Hostess of the Lion. Of descriptive passages, his pictures, "The Sea in a Calm," and the evening view from "The Upland Hamlets," though not perhaps the best he has ever written, are among the best.

> " Then the broad bosom of the ocean keeps
> An equal motion ; swelling as it sleeps,
> Then slowly sinking, curling to the strand,
> Faint, lazy waves o'ercreep the rigid sand,
> Or tap the tarry boat with gentle blow,
> And back return in silence, smooth and slow."

"The Tales," or " Tales in Verse," published in August 1812, are twenty-one in number. But none of them, I think, possesses quite the same beauty as either the " Borough" or the " Parish Register." " The Parting Hour," and the " Mother," are the two in which Crabbe's higher powers are most discernible. His lighter humour plays agreeably over the "Widow's Tale" and the "Frank Courtship ; " and the " Patron " is very interesting, for the reason to be found above.* " The Parting Hour " is a tale much resembling that of " Enoch Arden," though the couple are not married when Allen goes upon his travels. He is absent more than twenty years, and marries a Spanish girl in the West Indies, with whom he lives long and happily, and from whom he is at last torn away by the Inquisition. Wandering back to England in broken health, he finds Judith still unmarried. Both are now old, and she becomes his nurse and companion. And though he still sees in dreams his wife and his children, and his lost home in the tropics, and retains all his affection for them, she does not resent his

* See page 41.

feelings, but feels genuine grief and compassion for him. The story of the "Mother" is the common story of a broken heart, yet the death-bed of Lucy is described in such touching lines, as to rob the scene of all that is commonplace or hackneyed.

"Tales of the Hall," published in June 1819, seven years after the "Tales in Verse," represent the third and last period of Crabbe's poetical fecundity. The plan of the poem is different from that of the preceding ones, and boasts of greater unity and cohesion. Two brothers, parted early in life, pursue divergent careers, and are brought together again under circumstances very happily conceived. George, the elder, is adopted by an uncle in London, goes into his counting-house, experiences an early disappointment in love, and settles down into a money-making bachelor, though retaining, at the same time, all his natural kindness of heart. He amasses a large fortune, and returns to his native village, where he buys the Hall, an estate which the extravagance of its then owner has compelled him to sell. He finds one or two old friends still alive, and among others he recognises an old school-fellow in the Rector of the parish, whom he had not seen since they sat upon the same form at school, and with whom he now sits upon the same bench of magistrates. When George went to London Richard was left at home with his mother—not in the best circumstances—by whom, for seven years of his boyhood, he was allowed to run wild. Afterwards, for this part of the story is not very clear, he seems to have enlisted in the army, to have distinguished himself in the Peninsular War, and to have retired with the rank of captain. Richard was the rolling-stone who gathered

no moss, and when the story opens, is living in England
with a wife and children, finding some difficulty in
making both ends meet. His brother hears of him and
invites him to the Hall, where he is introduced to the
Rector, and for eight days the three amuse each other
over George's old port with relating their respective
adventures and experiences. Richard here gives that
description of his boyhood and self-education which so
delighted Cardinal Newman, and of which it is now time
that I should give the reader a specimen :—

> "I sought the town, and to the ocean gave
> My mind and thoughts, as restless as the wave ;
> Where crowds assembled I was sure to run,
> Heard what was said, and mused on what was done ;
> Attentive, listening in the moving scene,
> And often wondering what the men could mean.
> When ships at sea made signals of their need,
> I watched on shore the sailors and their speed :
> Mixed in their act, nor rested till I knew
> Why they were call'd, and what they had to do.
> Whatever business in the past was done,
> I, without call, was with the busy one :
> Not daring question, but with open ear
> And greedy spirit ever bent to hear.

> " What wondrous things in foreign parts they saw,
> Lands without bounds and people without law ;
> No ships were wrecked upon that fatal beach,
> But I could give the luckless tale of each.

> " I sought the men returned from regions cold,
> The frozen straits where icy mountains rolled ;
> Some I could win to tell me serious tales
> Of boats uplifted by enormous whales,
> Or when harpooned how swiftly through the sea
> The wounded monsters with the cordage flee.

" I loved to walk were none had walk'd before,
About the rocks that ran about the shore ;
Or far beyond the sight of man to stray,
And take my pleasure when I lost my way ;
For then 'twas mine to trace the hilly heath,
And all the mossy moor that lies beneath ;
Here had I favourite stations, where I stood
And heard the murmurs of the ocean-flood ;
With not a sound beside, except when flew
Aloft the lapwing or the grey curlew.

" Pleasant it was to see the sea-gulls strive
Against the storm, or in the ocean dive
With eager scream, or when they dropping gave
Their closing wings, to sail upon the wave ;
Then as the wind and waters rag'd around,
And breaking billows mixed their deafening sound,
They on the rolling deep, securely hung,
And calmly rode the restless waves among.
Nor pleased it less around me to behold,
Far up the beach, the yeasty sea-foam roll'd ;
Or from the shore upborne, to see on high,
Its frothy flakes in wild confusion fly ;
While the salt spray that clashing billows form,
Gave to the taste a feeling of the storm."

After this the Rector and his host describe what
they have witnessed, the one as a magistrate, the
other as a magistrate and a clergyman : the most
interesting story being that of the " Smugglers
and Poachers," full of deep, tragic, and pathetic
beauty. James, the gamekeeper, and Robert, the
poacher, are in love with the same girl, who, of course,
favours the more adventurous. Robert is caught after an
affray in which murder has been committed, and it seems
that nothing can save him from the gallows. James
promises Rachel that if she will marry him he will

save his brother's life, as he has power to keep the witnesses from appearing. Now comes a terrible struggle, both in the girl's own mind, and in that of her lover too. She visits him in prison, and we are allowed to see that she would herself rather see her lover die than become his brother's wife. But she leaves the decision to him. The end may be guessed. He feels, like Claudio, that life on any terms "is Paradise to what we fear of death." Rachel leaves him accordingly to become James's wife, and Robert escapes the gallows, only, however, to become a prey to raging jealousy and intense hatred of a brother who had exacted such a price for his deliverance. He resumes his old courses. In the middle of the night James is roused by the intelligence that poachers are among his pheasants. He sallies out, but is so long a time in returning, that his wife, impelled by she knows not what mysterious instinct, goes to seek for him in the dark, trembling at every step she takes, and at every rustle of the trees. What she finds, the reader has, perhaps, anticipated—the husband stark dead, and the lover just breathing his last, within a few yards of each other, though we are left to suppose that when the fatal shots were fired neither recognised his brother.

With this tale the visit concludes. Richard, a little annoyed that his brother takes leave of him so easily, allows his vexation to be seen. But George has a surprise in store for him. The next morning he rides part of the way with him, and just beyond the village shows him a pretty house and garden which he has bought for his use, and which he makes over to him as his absolute property. Richard has deserved this good luck, in his brother's estimation, by his demeanour as a guest, neither playing the poor relation, nor straining uneasily to assert his independence. The general effect of "The Tales of the Hall" is very pleasant. The machinery is ingenious; and there is just enough friction in the intercourse between the two brothers to give it an air of reality, without ever disturbing the general serenity of the picture.

The characters of the two brothers are admirably contrasted. Of George, the elder, we are told:—

> "Time, thought, and trouble made the man appear—
> By nature shrewd—sarcastic and severe;
> Still he was one whom those who fully knew,
> Esteemed and trusted, one correct and true;
> All on his word with surety might depend:
> Kind as a man and faithful as a friend,
> But him the many knew not."

> "Through ways more rough had fortune Richard led,
> The world he traversed was the book he read;
> Hence clashing notions and opinions strange
> Lodged in his mind, all liable to change.
> By nature generous, open, daring, free,
> The vice he hated was hypocrisy;
> Religious notions in her latter years
> His mother gave, admonish'd by her fears;
> To these he added, as he chanced to read
> A pious work or learn a Christian creed:
> He heard the preacher by the highway side
> The Church's teacher and the meeting's guide;
> And, mixing all their matters in his brain,
> Distilled a something he could ill explain,
> But still it served him for his daily use,
> And kept his lively passions from abuse."

When Crabbe died he left behind him, in MSS., a series of stories, which he thought would be sufficient to fill another volume. "Several persons of the highest eminence in literature," we are told, had read them in MS., and his sons conceived, therefore, that they should only be carrying out their father's wishes, without injury to his reputation, by including them in an edition of his works. The "Posthumous Tales" are twenty-two in number, and contain much that all the admirers of Crabbe will read with pleasure. In the "Boat Race," a story of wreck and sudden death, he is still the master of all that raises horror, anguish, and despair. The very pretty tale of "The Ancient Mansion" is full of a melancholy pathos. And the "Dean's Lady" is a lively satire on a dethroned blue stocking, who, having flourished greatly in her husband's life-time, finds after his death that the admiring circle who surrounded her were drawn thither as much by the fame of the Dean's cook, as by the fascinations of her own wit.

Of the other pieces in heroic verse which are published among Crabbe's poems, "Inebriety" and "The Candidate," written before he was known, show at what an early age he had obtained a mastery over the mechanical part of his profession. These I have already noticed.

The "Birth of Flattery" was published with the "Parish Register" in 1807. Flattery is the daughter of Poverty and Cunning. She is endowed by the fairies with magic charms. But a wicked spirit, whose name is Envy, decrees that they shall be her shame rather than her glory. The fairies, however, are not to be beaten, and they send Simulation to instruct her how to counteract the curse of Envy. It is not the name that shall be shameful. Flattery, when called by any other name, will be welcomed and honoured, and so it turned out—

> "Thus on her name, though all disgrace attend,
> In every creature she beholds a friend."

"Flirtation," published in 1816, is a dialogue between two young ladies, without either wit or novelty—perhaps the poet's only failure.

Crabbe's lyrical pieces shew that his genius was equally well adapted for that form of composition. In the "Ancient Mansion," a piece of this kind is introduced, which possesses great sweetness. The poet is wandering in the neighbourhood of an ancient hall, which he remembers long ago buried in venerable woods. He encounters an old man and his grand-daughter, who tells him of all the changes that have taken place.

> "And thus with gentle voice he spoke—
>   'Come lead me, lassie, to the shade,
> Where willows grow beside the brook :
>   For well I know the sound it made
> When dashing o'er the stony rill,
> It murmured to St. Osyth's mill.'
>
> The lass replied, 'The trees are fled,
> They've cut the brook a straighter bed :
> No shades the present lords allow,
> The miller only murmurs now ;
> The waters now the mill forsake,
> And form a pond they call a lake.'
>
> 'Then, lassie, lead thy grandsire on,
>   And to the holy water bring ;
> A cup is fastened to the stone,
>   And I would taste the healing spring

That soon its rocky cist forsakes,
And green its mossy passage makes.'

' The holy spring is turned aside,
The rock is gone, the stream is dried ;
The plough has levell'd all around,
And here is now no holy ground.' "

The "World of Dreams" has less merit. But "Sir Eustace Grey" and the " Hall of Justice" are pitched in a higher key, and show Crabbe at his very best. The first was written at Muston in the winter of 1804–5, during a great snow-storm ; and I give Crabbe's own account of it. " In the story of ' Sir Eustace Grey,' an attempt is made to describe the wanderings of a mind first irritated by the consequences of error and misfortune, and afterwards soothed by a species of enthusiastic conversion, still keeping him insane—a task very difficult ; and, if the presumption of the attempt may find pardon, it will not be refused to the failure of the poet. It is said of Shakspeare, respecting madness—

' In that circle none dare walk but he ;'

yet be it granted to one, who dares not to pass the boundary fixed for common minds, at least to step near to the tremendous verge, and form some idea of the terrors that are stalking in the interdicted space."

In the "Hall of Justice," we have a gipsy woman brought up before the magistrate, charged with stealing food, and she obtains permission to relate the story of her life to him. It is a shocking tale of incest, jealousy, and parricide, but it is written with marvellous power, albeit with great simplicity ; and I think the warmest admirers of Wordsworth must admit that he has met his match here. Sir Walter Scott applies the following stanza to the death-bed of Meg Merrilees :—

> " For, though seduced and led astray,
>   Thou'st travelled far, and wandered long;
>   Thy God hath seen thee all the way,
>   And all the turns that led thee wrong."

Besides the above, Crabbe published a number of occasional pieces, some of which had been written in the Duchess of Rutland's album. Of them, the best, I think, is one entitled "Storm and Calm," intended to illustrate the ease which a lover experiences when he has got rid of his passion, and the dulness which he suffers soon afterwards for the want of it. The thought is not new, but the verses are both polished and vigorous.

CHAPTER VIII.

WE have now to examine Crabbe's poems more particularly under the several heads of the subject matter of which they are composed, the construction of the tales and narratives introduced in them, the power which they exercise over the reader, the moral they convey, and, lastly, the language and versification in which they are expressed. Byron, writing to Murray in 1819, says—" Crabbe's the man—but he has got a coarse, impracticable subject." And Gifford, reviewing "The Borough," remarks that "if the checks of fancy and taste be removed from poetry, and admission be granted to images of whatever description, provided they have the passport of reality, it is not easy to tell at which point the line of exclusion should be drawn, or why it should be drawn at all." The answer is that the instinct of a true poet will tell him where to draw it. But Gifford and Byron, no doubt, express what was a very general opinion about Crabbe—namely, that the scenes and the persons to which he introduces us are too mean and vulgar to be proper subjects for poetry. In reply to this objection I think it is enough to point out that there is an essential distinction between things which are mean in themselves and things which are mean only by reason of their surrounding circumstances. Johnson rightly ridiculed the line, "Now, Muse, let's sing of rats." But real passion can surely never be mean, whether we seek it in the back slums of dirty seaports, or in the wreck of royal houses, *inter veterum penetralia regum.* The reader will hardly need to be reminded of the fisherman's cottage in the "Antiquary," and the profoundly touching scene of human sorrow which is there displayed to us, surrounded by all that is mean, sordid, and squalid. Crabbe's first object was the exhibition of human nature and human suffering, and if he ever takes us into scenes of meanness and squalor without this object in view, and merely to show how well he can paint the broken pots and pans, the drunken ruffians, and slatternly viragos, then he is amenable to Gifford's criticism. And I do not say that he never does this. To enlarge on disagreeable details at too great length is, unquestionably, his besetting sin. Hazlitt says, wittily, of Crabbe, that he "turns diseases to commodity." And this is true. But Hazlitt had no insight into Crabbe's moral purpose ; and does not seem to see that he was a satirist first, and a poet afterwards. "Our English Juvenal," Scott calls him ; and if this view of his literary character be correct, then Hazlitt's criticism, and, in some degree, Gifford's also, is beside the mark.

Both blame him for rejecting those "illusions," which, in the judgment of both, are the proper province of poetry. "He sets out professing to overturn the poetical theory of rural life, the glory and the dream, as it has been since the days of Theocritus. Then, why not lay aside the cap and bells at once? why not insist on the unwelcome reality in plain prose ? "* The answer is, that Crabbe is a satirist, and that satire, by common consent, is capable of metrical expression. Gifford, I think, is Crabbe's most judicious critic, as he fairly discriminates between his blemishes and his beauties. Jeffrey's eulogy and Hazlitt's censure are alike too sweeping. The truth, on the whole, seems to be that Crabbe's cardinal defect was an imperfectly cultivated taste, which prevented him at times from seeing when he was overstepping the line between such painful and repulsive topics as are inseparable from his subject matter, and those which are wantonly disgusting. The fault is a grave one; but does not affect the singular power with which he depicts human emotions, and lays open the secret springs and hypocritical pretences of human conduct.

As a mine of .character, Crabbe tells us that he preferred the middle-classes. " I have," says he, "chiefly, if not exclusively, taken my subjects and characters from that order of society where the least display of vanity is generally to be found, which is placed between the humble and the great. It is in this class of mankind that more originality of character, more variety of fortune, will be met with ; because, on the one hand, they do not live in the eye of the world, and therefore are not kept in awe by the dread of observation and indecorum : neither, on the other, are they debarred by their want of means from the cultivation of mind and the pursuits of wealth and ambition, which are necessary to the development of character displayed in the variety of situations to which this class is liable."

* Hazlitt.

That less vanity is to be found in the middle-classes than in either the upper or the lower is an assertion I should hesitate to accept. The rest of the passage is, upon the whole, I think, true, though it is more true of the country than it is of the town, where there must necessarily be some kind of public opinion to which not even the most hardened are absolutely indifferent.

Of human nature and of human life Crabbe did not take a flattering view, though efforts have been made to represent it in different colours. In a letter written to his son, Joanna Baillie says :—" I have sometimes remarked that, when a good or generous action has been much praised, he would say in a low voice, as to himself, something that insinuated a more mingled and worldly cause for it. But this never, as it would have done from any other person, gave the least offence ; for you felt quite assured, as he uttered it, that it proceeded from a sagacious observance of mankind, and was spoken in sadness, not in the spirit of satire." That Crabbe's satire had more of sadness than of malice in it is quite true. But that is nothing to the purpose ; it is satire all the same. Like many other men, time, prosperity, and public favour taught him to think better of the world ; and in " The Tales of the Hall" we see a much fuller recognition of the better side of human nature than we find in his earlier productions. But the habit recorded by Joanna Bailie, who knew him in his advanced years, shows that his original prepossessions still clung to him, and that when he heard of a good action his first impulse was to find a bad motive for it.

In his treatment of the lower and middle-classes, it is

instructive, as I have already said, to compare Crabbe with George Eliot, for they both drew from the same source, and both depend on the deeper springs of human action for awakening our interest in their characters. But as regards external conditions, there is one point on which they differ, with which I have frequently been struck. In all George Eliot's tales of rural life no suggestion escapes her of that extreme depression among the agricultural poor, on which Crabbe is so eloquent. She had lived among them in her youth, and knew all their traditions, prejudices, and grievances. It is curious that she drops no hint of any misery or discontent prevailing among them—says nothing of their hardships or their penury, their stinted meals and fireless grates—of the aches and pains which await them in their old age, and the workhouse which receives them in the end. I have often remarked on the absence of any such topics in George Eliot's writings, and a reperusal of Crabbe has made it seem more singular than ever.

Of the construction and incidents of Crabbe's Tales there is little to say. They usually narrate the fortunes or adventures of not more than two or three persons in a simple and direct manner, independently of mystery or catastrophe. The principal exception to this rule is in the "Tale of Smugglers and Poachers," in "Tales of the Hall," and perhaps the scheme of the two brothers, on which the whole series rests, may be thought another. Yet Crabbe is essentially a story-teller. Pope's characters are either portraits—rarely drawn, no doubt—or else pegs on which to hang certain illustrations of human nature, exquisitely painted, but not representing living, breathing human beings. Nobody, for instance, can be interested in Sir Balaam as an individual, however we admire him as a type. But Crabbe *interests* us in his characters. We follow their footsteps with curiosity, and make their troubles and successes our own.

That Crabbe was possessed, in no common degree, of that peculiar power by which compassion, horror, scorn, despair, and indignation are excited, is sufficiently proved, I think, by the foregoing extracts. Wordsworth says that these feelings are less easily aroused in us by verse than by prose ; and he compares the most tragic scenes in Shakespeare with the sorrows of Richardson's " Clarissa," and says that while we can read the former without any painful emotion, we shrink from returning to the latter a second time, in dread of its agitating effect. The remark is true ; and the reason given for it, namely, that the pleasure which we derive from verse com- position distracts our attention from the painful nature of the subject, is on the whole just. Yet Crabbe has levelled even these distinctions. For not all the beauty of the verse can enable us to read the work- house scene in " The Village," the mother's death in the " Parish Register," the wreck in the " Boat Race," or the gipsy woman's story in the " Hall of Justice," without sensations being raised in us which we do not care to experience too often.

The moral inculcated by Crabbe is simple. He shows, as Mary Leadbeater has observed, the real consequences of vice—here again resembling George Eliot—and rebuking the insidious voice, which whispers to every man and woman on the verge of doing wrong, " Thou shalt not surely die." Thackeray laughs at this simple morality, as he calls it. Jack was a good boy and had plum-cake : Harry was a bad boy, and was eaten by wild beasts. But I don't know what can be substituted for it. Virtue, it is true, is not always rewarded, nor vice punished, in this world. Neither do industry and frugality invariably make a man rich, nor idleness and self-indulgence poor. But all we can do is to show that virtue, industry, and frugality are the best policy on the whole. Probability, the guide of life, as Butler says, is in their favour. And in matters of action, the balance of probability, though it weigh down the scale only by the weight of a feather, is enough to determine us. Crabbe shows that impatience, imprudence, vanity, passion, and a selfish disregard of others, no less than down-right violence and crime, often land us in very pitiable predicaments.

Crabbe was ridiculed in "Rejected Addresses," where he is called Pope in worsted stockings. The satire is mis-directed, though the parody, as Crabbe himself allowed, is excellent. To my mind Crabbe, though the last of Pope's school, and specially interesting on that account, is very unlike Pope. His turn of thought is not the same. He looks out upon the world with different eyes, and, what is more, he is guilty of faults of style, and breaches of good taste, at which Pope would have shuddered. The great fault of his versification is a too frequent straining after antithesis, when the sense is not improved by it, and the effect is purely verbal. Examples of what I mean are the following :—

> " Here are no wheels for either wool or flax,
>   But packs of cards, made up of various packs."

A lady's brother interferes to prevent a gentleman from trifling with his sister's affections—

> " Yet others tell the captain fixed thy doubt,
>   He'd call thee brother, or he'd call thee out."

Of Lucy Collins, captivated by footman Daniel in his smart livery, we are told—

> " But from that day, the fatal day, she spied
>   The pride of Daniel, Daniel was her pride."

Of Abel Keene—

> " A quiet, simple man was Abel Keene, ·
>   He meant no harm, nor did he often mean."

On couplets of this kind—and I have not given the worst specimens—the author of " Rejected Addresses " fastened greedily; and one wonders that one who generally wrote so well as Crabbe should ever have condescended to such absurdities. Another great blemish in his versification is his too frequent use of the Alexandrine.

The parody of Crabbe in the " Rejected Addresses " was considered by Jeffrey the best thing which they contained, because it was an imitation not only of Crabbe's mannerism, but also of his mental peculiarities. I do not see, however, that the parody of Crabbe is superior in this respect to many others in the volume. Crabbe, it is needless to say, almost invited parody of a certain kind. His puns and iterations, often without wit or point, could be copied with very little ingenuity; and this is nearly all that is done in " The Theatre." A boy drops his hat fro: ᵗʰᵉ gallery, a string of pocket-handkerchiefs is let down, by which the hat is drawn up again.   The owner

" Regained his felt, and felt what he regained."

Imitations like this may be manufactured by the score by anyone who possesses that particular kind of ingenuity. Against Smith's general estimate of Crabbe I have already entered a sufficient protest.   The jester of the period, who made fun of these external oddities, was totally unable to appreciate the real feeling, the contempt for folly, selfishness, and hypocrisy, which lay beneath the surface.

But a still greater drawback to the enjoyment of Crabbe's poetry is the fault to which we have already referred—the bad taste which mars some of his finest passages.   One can never be sure of him.   As we move slowly through some beautiful description, or some melancholy tragedy, enchanted by the sweetness and fidelity of the one, or the pathos and passion of the other, we are always apt to be tripped up by some literary *gaucherie* which interrupts the illusion, and brings us down again to the common day.   I have already quoted the description of the ruined monastery.   But I did not quote one couplet of it, which fortunately comes near the end, or else it would spoil the whole.   Amid a crowd of beautiful images and romantic associations which the poet brings together in this passage, we read—

" That oxen low, where monks retired to eat."

This is shocking.   What follows is, if possible, even worse.   I have quoted the " Felon's Dream," a passage dark with all the horrors of death and hell, and looking all the more dreadful for the flash of dream-light thrown across them. Yet the poet must needs tell us that when the sleeping criminal saw his native village, he saw too

> " The house, the chamber, where he once arrayed
> His youthful person."

Again, in the description of the girl taking leave of her lover who is going to sea, and returns only to die in her arms, the care which she bestowed upon his wardrobe is one of the principal particulars—

> " White was his better linen, and his check
> Was made more trim than any on the deck."

It is no pleasure to multiply examples of this unlucky deficiency, or many might be given, some far more ludicrous than the above. It is more interesting to speculate on the source of this singular anomaly. Crabbe, it is said, was to the last, inaccessible to the charms of order, congruity, and regularity. He has satirised the love of order in the "Learned Boy." He had no ear for music, and no eye for proportion or perspective. He did not understand architecture, and, except for the general effect, would have seen little difference between Westminster Abbey and Buckingham Palace. He liked to accumulate specimens of insects, grasses, and fossils; but he derived no pleasure from classifying them according to their species. Weeds and flowers of the most diverse characters all grew together in his garden in wild confusion. It was enough that they were there. To arrange them according to their kinds, or to mingle their various hues so as to produce the best effect, was what never occured to him for a moment. We see the same tendency at work in his poetry. His descriptions are often overcharged from the desire to omit nothing, and remind us of the shepherd who thought that a landscape painting ought to be as complete as an ordnance map. Thus we can understand that he might have been comparatively indifferent to the frequency with which incongruous ideas and conflicting moods refuse to blend together in his poetry, and quite unconscious of the shock which the intrusion of commonplace or vulgar thoughts into passages of highly-wrought sentiment is calculated to inflict on palates of greater literary nicety.

His son and biographer laments his father's want of taste, and tells us even that he had little appreciation of "what the painter's eye considers as the beauties of landscape." This is very singular, when we consider his power of describing natural beauty. He was certainly one of the closest observers of nature, and especially of the sea in all its moods, which our literature can show. Some of his little sea pieces are decidedly picturesque, and this effect could hardly be produced by one who had no eye for colour, for light, shade, or movement. The truth is, that the quality in which Crabbe's poetry is deficient is elegance, admirably described by Johnson as the beauty of propriety. The picturesque may be produced by a single happy touch, as in the lines already quoted descriptive of the waves in a calm :—

> "That tap the tarry boat with gentle blow,
> And back return in silence smooth and slow."

But elegance is the result of selection, combination, and arrangement ; all, in fact, that in a painting is called composition—the beauty of order, the beauty of harmony. To accuse Crabbe in general terms, therefore, of a want of taste, is to bring too sweeping a charge against him. His taste was imperfect, but it was rather in the discriminative than the appreciative faculty of taste that the defect lay. Hence the uncertainty of which I have already spoken—the constant doubt in reading his finest passages, whether we may not suddenly stumble over some utterly inappropriate image, or some wretched triviality, which destroys half the effect of it. It is not purple patches that offend the reader in Crabbe, but the beads of clay strung at intervals upon the chain of pearls.

It is remarkable that Crabbe's versification grew worse as he grew older. In his three earliest poems there are passages which have really some pretensions to elegance, the result, I suppose, of assiduous labour when he was just fresh from the study of Pope. In his later works such passages grow less and less frequent, though still occasionally to be met with. When asked by Rogers what was the reason for this difference, Crabbe very candidly replied that in his youthful compositions he was on his promotion, but that when his popularity was assured, he no longer felt it necessary to take so much trouble. No real lover of style as such would ever have given this reply.

With Crabbe, as I have said, the old dynasty of poets, who ruled English literature for a hundred years, came to an end, amid the murmured regrets of many who, for a long time, refused allegiance to its successors. That controversy is over now ; and the heroic school of poetry is as dead as the house of Stuart. But a peculiar, and even a romantic, interest attaches to its

last representative, who connects the age of Johnson
with the age of Tennyson, and prolonged nearly to the
reign of Victoria the literary form and method which
ripened in the reign of Anne. Crabbe, however, could
not seclude himself from the operation of the new forces
at work within his own era; and the distinctive mark of
his poetry is the attempt to marry the new ideas of a
revolutionary epoch, which was just beginning, to
the old style of a strictly conservative period, which
was just ending. He, in fact, accomplished the
great feat of pouring new wine into old bottles, if
not without occasional breakage, yet, on the whole,
with eminent success; and those who can admire
his poetry for nothing else may at least admire it as
a wonderful *tour de force*. But Crabbe has far other
claims upon us than those of a dexterous versifier,
subduing to the heroic metre thoughts, scenes, and
actions which had hitherto rejected it. He is a
great moral writer, and one of the greatest English
satirists. He was almost the first to paint in colours
that will last the tragedy of humble life; and though
inferior both in humour and psychological insight to
George Eliot, he has anticipated her in drawing from
the short and simple annals of the poor the materials of
domestic dramas almost as touching as her own. In
his knowledge of human nature, in the ordinary sense of
the term, he was quite her equal, and I think Pope's
superior; while it must also be remembered that he too
anticipated George Eliot in discerning the rich harvest
of literary wealth to be gathered from the middle-classes,
or those which, a hundred years ago, lay between the
gentry and the tradespeople, and supplied the authoress

of *Adam Bede* with her Tulliver and Pullets, which will live for ever with Jane Austen's Norrises and Eltons, taken from the class just above them.

Crabbe came upon the stage at a lucky moment for his own immediate popularity; but I am not so sure that it was a lucky one for his popularity with posterity. The combination of qualities which made his poetry so attractive to men like Jeffrey and Byron owed its charm to the fact that it represented a transition period, when the old and new styles were just melting into each other. But the general public, I think, has, upon the whole, preferred to take them separately, thinking Pope very good, and Wordsworth very good, but not caring much about the mixture. What helped Crabbe so much with the critics of his own time has rather been against him in ours, and has interfered with the due appreciation of his real greatness, which is quite independent of rhymes and metres. We have only to read the "Hall of Justice" to see how near he was to what is called the modern spirit. Change the metre, and we can imagine its occurring in the latest volume of Lord Tennyson. It is curious, too, that when Crabbe uses any lyric metre, he is totally free from all those puerile conceits which disfigure his heroics. Nobody would ever dare to parody Crabbe's lyrics; and it may be a question after all whether he was not doing some violence to the natural bent of his genius in resolving to be a disciple of Pope.

However this may be, he has left behind him a body of poetry, which, whether we regard the delineation of manners, the knowledge of character, the strength of passion, or the beauty of description combined in it, need not shrink from comparison with works of which the fame is much more widely extended. Dryden, Pope, Goldsmith, Johnson, to say nothing of the later poets, each, no doubt, excelled Crabbe in some of these particulars; but they are not united to the same extent in any one of them. This distinction does not necessarily make him either so delightful a companion, or so great a poet, as those that I have named. But it qualifies him to take rank with the best of them as a Great Writer.

FINIS.

INDEX.

———◆◆———

BIBLIOGRAPHY.

BY

JOHN P. ANDERSON

(British Museum).

I. WORKS.
II. APPENDIX—
    Biography, Criticism, etc.
    Magazine Articles.

III. CHRONOLOGICAL LIST OF
    WORKS.

I. WORKS.

Poems. London, 1807, 8vo.
——Second edition. London, 1808, 8vo.
——Third edition. London, 1808, 8vo.
——Sixth edition. 2 vols. London, 1812, 8vo.
——Eighth edition. London, 1816, 12mo.
——Another edition. 7 vols. London, 1822, 8vo.
——Another edition. 5 vols. London, 1823, 8vo.
——Another edition. 8 vols. London, 1823, 12mo.
——Another edition. The Poetical Works of George Crabbe. Paris [1829 ?], 4to.

——Another edition. With his letters and journals, and his life by his son [G. Crabbe]. 8 vols. London, 1834, 8vo.
—— ——Prospectus of the first complete and uniform edition of the Poetical Works of the Rev. George Crabbe, with his letters and journals, etc. London, 1833, 8vo.
——Another edition. 2 vols. in 1. London, 1835, 16mo.
——Another edition. With an essay on his genius and writings. London, 1837, 16mo.
——The Life and Poetical Works of George Crabbe. Edited by his son [G. Crabbe]. Complete in 1 vol. London, 1847, 8vo.

The Life and Poetical Works of George Crabbe. New edition. London, 1854, 8vo.
There is also an engraved title-page, dated 1851.
——Another edition. The Poetical Works of George Crabbe, with life. Edinburgh [1855], 8vo.
——New edition, illustrated. With a life [by W. R.]. (*Routledge's British Poets.*) London, 1858, 8vo.
——Another edition. Illustrated. 2 pts. London [1873], 8vo.
——Another edition. With life, etc. Edinburgh [1881], 8vo.
Part of "The Landscape Series of Poets."
——Poems: The Village. The Library. The Newspaper. The Parish Register. (*Cassell's National Library.*) London, 1886, 8vo.

The Borough:—a poem, in twenty-four letters. London, 1810, 8vo.
——Fourth edition. 2 vols. London, 1812, 8vo.
——Sixth edition. London, 1816, 12mo.
——Another edition. (*The Universal Library. Poetry,* vol. iii.) London [1854], 8vo.
The Candidate, a poetical epistle to the authors of the *Monthly Review.* London, 1780, 4to.
Character of Lord Robert Manners. (*Annual Register,* vol. xxvi., 1783, pp. 35-40.)
Correspondence of George Crabbe and Mrs. Leadbeater. (*The Leadbeater Papers,* vol. ii., pp. 335-403.) London, 1862, 8vo.
A discourse [on 2 Cor. i., 9.] read in the chapel at Belvoir Castle after the funeral of the Duke of Rutland. London, 1788, 4to.

——Another edition. Dublin, 1788, 8vo.
Inebriety: a poem, in three parts. Ipswich, 1775, 8vo.
The Library: a poem. London, 1781, 4to.
——Second edition. London, 1783, 4to.
Natural History of the Vale of Belvoir. (*Nichol's History of the County of Leicester,* vol. i., pt. 1, pp. cxci.-cciii.) London, 1795, fol.
The Newspaper: a poem. London, 1785, 4to.
The Parish Register, and other poems, by George Crabbe. And the Sabbath and other poems, by J. Grahame, with memoirs of the authors. London [1863], 16mo.
The Parish Register appeared originally in the 1807 edition of Crabbe's Poems.
Posthumous Sermons, edited by J. D. Hastings. London, 1850, 8vo.
Tales. London, 1812, 8vo.
——Fifth edition. London, 1814, 8vo.
——Another edition. (*The Universal Library. Poetry,* vol. iii.) London, 1854, 8vo.
Tales of the Hall. 2 vols. London, 1819, 8vo.
——Readings in Crabbe. "Tales of the Hall." [With an introduction by Edward Fitzgerald.] London, 1882, 8vo.
The Variation of Public Opinion and Feelings considered, as it respects Religion; a Sermon [on 1 Cor. x., 6.]. London, 1817, 8vo.
The Village; a Poem. In two books. London, 1783, 4to.
——Another edition. With prefatory and explanatory notes.

(*Blackie's School Classics.*) London, 1879, 16mo.

Cullings from Crabbe, with a memoir of his life and notices of his writings. Bath, 1832, 12mo.

Summer Scenes ; a series of photographs . . . with appropriate selections from the poems of . . . Crabbe, etc. By Birket Foster. London, 1867, 4to.

II. APPENDIX.

BIOGRAPHY, CRITICISM, ETC.

Balfour, Alexander. — Characters omitted in Crabbe's Parish Register ; with other tales. Edinburgh, 1825, 12mo.

Belfast, Earl of.—Poets and Poetry of the Nineteenth Century. A course of lectures, etc. London, 1852, 8vo.
> Crabbe, pp. 253-263.

Bransby, James Hews. — Brief notices of the late Rev. George Crabbe, in a letter to the editor of the *Carnarvon Herald.* Carnarvon, 1832, 8vo.

British Poets. — Biographical Sketches of eminent British Poets, etc. Dublin, 1851, 8vo.
> George Crabbe, pp. 454-472.

Cunningham, Allan. — Biographical and critical history of the British Literature of the last fifty years. Paris, 1834, 8vo.
> Crabbe, pp. 25-32.

Cunningham, George G.—Lives of eminent and illustrious Englishmen, etc. 8 vols. Glasgow, 1835-7, 8vo.
> George Crabbe, vol. viii., pp. 416-423.

Devey, J.—A comparative estimate of modern English poets. London, 1873, 8vo.
> Crabbe, pp. 368-375.

Giles, Henry.—Lectures and Essays. 2 vols. Boston, 1850, 8vo.
> Crabbe, vol. i., pp. 45-92.

Gilfillan, George.—A Second Gallery of Literary Portraits. Edinburgh, 1850, 8vo.
> George Crabbe, pp. 61-80.

Grinsted, T. P.—Relics of Genius: visits to the last homes of poets, etc. London, 1859, 8vo.
> George Crabbe, pp. 249-252.

Hazlitt, William.—The Spirit of the Age ; or contemporary portraits. London, 1825, 8vo.
> Mr. Campbell and Mr. Crabbe, pp. 185-205.

Jeffrey, Francis. — Contributions to the *Edinburgh Review.* London, 1853, 8vo.
> Crabbe's Poems, pp. 482-491 ; The Borough, pp. 491-503 ; Tales, pp. 503-515 ; Tales of the Hall, pp. 515-526.

Lives.—Lives of the Illustrious. (The Biographical Magazine.) London, 1854, 8vo.
> George Crabbe, vol. vi., pp. 87-96.

Moore, Thomas.—Memoirs, Journal, and Correspondence of Thomas Moore. 8 vols. London, 1853-56, 8vo.
> Numerous references to Crabbe.

Oliphant, Mrs. M. O.—The Literary History of England, etc. 3 vols. London, 1882, 8vo.
> George Crabbe, vol. i., pp. 184-216.

Poets.—The Living Poets of England, etc. 2 vols. Paris, 1827, 8vo.
> George Crabbe, vol. i., pp. 175-278.

Smith, H. and J.—Rejected Addresses. London, 1812, 12mo.
> Parody on Crabbe, pp. 101-109.

Stephen, Leslie. — Hours in a Library. (Second Series.) London, 1876, 8vo.
> Crabbe's Poetry, pp. 242-289 ; appeared originally in the *Cornhill Magazine,* vol. xxx., 1874.

Stephen Leslie.—Crabbe. (*Dictionary of National Biography*, vol. xii.) London, 1887, 8vo.

Tuckerman, Henry T.—Thoughts on the Poets. New York, 1848, 8vo.

    Crabbe, pp. 122-136.

Ward, Thomas Humphry.—The English Poets. Selections, with critical introductions, etc. 4 vols. London, 1883-4, 8vo.

    George Crabbe, by W. J. Courthope, vol. iii., pp. 581-595.

MAGAZINE ARTICLES.

Crabbe, George. Tait's Edinburgh Magazine, by George Gilfillan, vol. 14, 2nd Series, 1847, pp. 141-147; same article, Littell's Living Age, vol. 11, pp. 1-9. — Sharpe's London Journal, by F. Lawrence, vol. 12, 1850, pp. 21-28; same article, Eclectic Magazine, vol. 21, pp. 64-73.—People's Journal, vol. 11, 1851, p. 1, etc.—Eclectic Magazine (from the Leisure Hour), vol. 2, N.S. 1865, pp. 343-349.—Art Journal, by S. C. Hall, 1865, pp. 373, 374; same article, Eclectic Magazine, vol. 3, N.S., pp. 216-219, and Every Saturday, vol. 1, p. 48, etc.—Atlantic Monthly, by G. E. Woodberry, vol. 45, 1880, pp. 624-629.

——*The Borough.* Quarterly Review, by W. Gifford, vol. 4, 1810, pp. 281-312.—Edinburgh Review, by F. Jeffrey, vol. 16, 1810, pp. 30-55.—Eclectic Review, vol. 6, 1810, pp. 546-561. —Christian Observer, vol. 10, 1811, pp. 502-511.

——*Life of.* New Monthly Magazine, vol. 4, 1816, pp. 511-517. —Quarterly Review, by J. G. Lockhart, vol. 50, 1834, pp.

Crabbe, George.

    468-508.—New England Magazine, vol. 8, 1835, pp. 215-219.

——*Life and Poems.* Eclectic Review, vol. 11, 3rd Series, 1834, pp. 253-278; vol. 12, 3rd Series, pp. 305-314.—Select Journal, vol. 4, 1834, p. 1, etc.— North American Review, by O. W. B Peabody, vol. 39, 1834, pp. 135-166.—Monthly Review, vol. 3, N. S., 1834, pp. 101-115. —Edinburgh Review, vol. 60, 1835, pp. 255-296.—Westminster Review, vol. 30, 1835, pp. 316-341.—New York Review, vol. 1, 1837, pp. 96, etc.— Methodist Quarterly Review, vol. 23, 1841, pp. 460-471, 514-534.—National Review, vol. 8, 1859, pp. 1-32; same article, Littell's Living Age, vol. 60, pp. 529-546.

——*Poems.* Edinburgh Review, by F. Jeffrey, vol. 12, 1808, pp. 131-151.—Eclectic Review, vol. 5, 1809, pp. 40-49.—London Magazine, vol. 3, 1821, pp. 484-490.—Littell's Museum of Foreign Literature, vol. 13, 1828, p. 625, etc.; vol. 22, p. 626, etc.; vol. 23, p. 132, etc.; vol. 24, p. 477, etc.; vol. 25, p. 579, etc.—Tait's Edinburgh Magazine, vol. 1, N.S., 1834, pp. 161-168.—St. James's Magazine, vol. 2, N.S., 1869, pp. 677-688. North American Review, by F. Sheldon, vol. 115, 1872, pp. 48-60. — Cornhill Magazine, by Leslie Stephen, vol 30, 1874, pp. 454-473; reprinted in "Hours in a Library," 1876; same article, Littell's Living Age, vol. 123, pp. 403-416.

——*Posthumous Tales.* Quarterly Review, by J. G. Lockhart, vol. 52. 1834, pp. 184-203.

Crabbe, George.
——*Tales.* Edinburgh Review, by F. Jeffrey, vol. 20, 1812, pp. 277-305.—Eclectic Review, vol. 8, 1812, pp, 1240-1253.
——*Tales of the Hall.* Edinburgh Review, by F. Jeffrey, vol. 32, 1819, pp. 118-148. — Blackwood's Edinburgh Magazine, vol. 5, 1819, pp. 469-483.—

Crabbe, George.
Monthly Review, vol. 90, N.S., 1819, pp. 225-238.—Christian Observer, vol. 18, 1819, pp. 650-668.—Eclectic Review, vol. 13, N.S., 1820, pp. 114-133.—Eclectic Magazine (from Saturday Review), vol. 63, 1864, pp. 416-420.

III. CHRONOLOGICAL LIST OF WORKS.